SO-ABP-844

DEMOCRACY, AMERICA, AND THE AGE OF GLOBALIZATION

Because political campaigns in the United States are privately funded, America's political system is heavily biased toward the interests of wealthy campaign contributors. As a result, government policies have largely ignored the growth in income inequality caused by technological change and economic globalization. This omission has been tolerated because most Americans do not actively support interventionist government policies. They believe that the government serves the interests of campaign donors rather than the public. This skepticism concerning the public sector's fairness must be overcome before effective programs to offset mounting inequality can be implemented. Though in recent years legislation to reform the financing of political campaigns has been adopted, private wealth continues to dominate the political process. Political cynicism therefore persists. A voluntary system of public funding of candidates for office is required to generate the trust in the public sector necessary to reverse the trend toward inequality.

Jay R. Mandle, currently W. Bradford Wiley Professor of Economics at Colgate University, has also taught at Temple University and the University of the West Indies. Mandle has been a Visiting Scholar at the Institute for Social Change at the University of California, Berkeley, and twice been a Fulbright Lecturer, once at the University of Guyana and once at Nankai University, China. Among his many publications, Professor Mandle recently published *Globalization and the Poor* (2003).

Democracy, America, and the Age of Globalization

Jay R. Mandle

Colgate University

CAMBRIDGE
UNIVERSITY PRESS

CAMBRIDGE UNIVERSITY PRESS
Cambridge, New York, Melbourne, Madrid, Cape Town, Singapore,
São Paulo, Delhi

Cambridge University Press
32 Avenue of the Americas, New York, NY 10013-2473, USA

www.cambridge.org
Information on this title: www.cambridge.org/9780521885898

© Jay R. Mandle 2008

This publication is in copyright. Subject to statutory exception
and to the provisions of relevant collective licensing agreements,
no reproduction of any part may take place without
the written permission of Cambridge University Press.

First published 2008

Printed in the United States of America

A catalog record for this publication is available from the British Library.

Library of Congress Cataloging in Publication Data
Mandle, Jay R.
Democracy, America, and the age of globalization / Jay R. Mandle.
p. cm.
Includes bibliographical references and index.
ISBN 978-0-521-88589-8 (hardback) – ISBN 978-0-521-71365-8 (pbk.)
1. Campaign funds – United States. 2. Income distribution – United States.
3. Globalization – Political aspects – United States. 4. United States –
Politics and government. I. Title.
JK1991.M26 2008
324.7′80973 – dc22 2007019988

ISBN 978-0-521-88589-8 hardback
ISBN 978-0-521-71365-8 paperback

Cambridge University Press has no responsibility for
the persistence or accuracy of URLs for external or
third-party Internet Web sites referred to in this publication
and does not guarantee that any content on such
Web sites is, or will remain, accurate or appropriate.

*To the student activists
who know Democracy Matters*

Contents

Preface

As an author, I have the good fortune to possess friends who are willing to tell me that my thoughts have not yet adequately cohered or that my manuscript is not yet a book. Indeed, for better or worse, I have four such friends: Paul Lyons, Mike Burke, Louis Ferleger, and Jon Mandle. All discussed the ideas in this study with me and read earlier versions of this book. All, at one time or another, made it clear to me that I had not yet accomplished what I had set out to do. For that I thank them.

My idea was to bring together two sets of issues: the problems caused by economic globalization and technological change, on the one hand, and those associated with the way we fund political campaigns, on the other hand. I wished to argue that there was a need to change the latter in order to solve the former. I wanted to reject neither the economic growth associated with market economies nor the goal of distributing the benefits of economic modernization fairly.

The dislocations caused by economic progress are real and substantial. But I believe that alleviating these problems does not require rejecting global market integration and technological change, much less a market-based economy. Rather, my hypothesis is that achieving a more egalitarian political process is the key to greater economic justice. To make this case, it was necessary for me to synthesize strands from a variety of disciplines: economics, of course, but also democratic theory, survey research, and even philosophic discourse. My problem was to blend all of these threads into a seamless whole. I have been fortunate that my editor at Cambridge, Lew Bateman, has encouraged this interdisciplinary effort.

In preparing this study, I benefited immensely from the fact that Colgate University granted me a one-year research leave of absence during the 2005–6 academic year. I particularly want to thank Patrick Kendall, an economist at the Caribbean Development Bank, for taking my classes during the time I was on that sabbatical. I also benefited from the opportunity to present the ideas in this study at seminars at Colgate University, Union College, the Richard A. Easterlin Conference at the University of Southern California, and in Australia at the University of New South Wales and the University of Sydney.

What I lost in terms of classroom stimulation, however, I was able in part to offset as a result of my interaction with the students who are members of the campus-based organization Democracy Matters, which I discuss in Chapter 7. These young political activists were always more than ready to challenge my arguments when I presented them. Their unshaken belief in the value of political equality – and therefore democratic processes – is inspiring and provided me with an important impetus to complete this study. In this, my adopted son, Adonal Foyle, played a critical role. There would be no Democracy Matters without him. Adonal demonstrates how it is possible to excel in a profession and, at the same time, be an active and effective participant in the process of democratic self-governance.

Finally, it is important for me to identify the role played by my wife, Joan Mandle, in the development of this project. She is a deep and true life partner. There is literally nothing in this book that is not at least in part hers. Over the years we have grown together, and this work is the result of that process.

I hope this study will contribute to what is already an intensifying discussion of how the United States can adjust to a world of rapid economic change. I would like it to be seen as weighing in on the side of the argument affirming that economic growth and economic equity are reconcilable objectives.

Introduction

Technological change and economic globalization are beneficial to the American economy as a whole but impose substantial costs as well. How those benefits and costs are distributed is determined by the country's political institutions. Globalization can become a source of economic renewal and advance for the people of this country. But the converse is also possible. And what is worse, at present that appears to be the more likely outcome. The inequality built into our politics makes it all too probable that technological advances and continued economic growth in today's poor countries will worsen the already too deep economic and social fissures present in American society.

The thesis presented in this book is that our political system is too biased toward the interests of wealthy campaign contributors to respond fairly to the problems that emerge from the new global economic order. My argument is that the kinds of policy interventions that could offset deepening domestic income inequality require an egalitarian politics, something

1

that we sadly lack today. The systematically unequal political process present in the United States cannot be expected to produce a just response to the inequities associated with globalization. The late John Rawls, the eminent theorist of justice, explains why this is so:

> the liberties protected by the principle of participation lose much of their value whenever those who have greater private means are permitted to use their advantages to control the course of public debate ... eventually these inequalities will enable those better situated to exercise a larger influence over the development of legislation. In due time they are likely to acquire a preponderant weight in settling social questions, at least in regard to those matters upon which they normally agree, which is to say in regard to those things that support their favored circumstances.[1]

An egalitarian political system would be one in which each voting-age citizen is able, if he or she wishes, to exercise meaningful political influence. The problem is that no one I know of has theorized about the financing of such a system. How much money would such a system cost, who would pay for it, and how would those funds be distributed? There is, of course, an abundant and useful journalistic and scholarly literature on the American system of privately funded elections, much of which emphasizes the political inequalities that are built

---

[1] John Rawls, *A Theory of Justice* (Cambridge MA: Harvard University Press, 1971), p. 225.

into it. But to my knowledge, no academic literature exists that analytically investigates the consequences of alternative systems of political finance and assesses the financing requirements of an egalitarian political system. Because of this void, little theoretical guidance is available to assist those who seek to make the political process more equal. With that the case, even Rawls was cautious in suggesting how to proceed. Because, Rawls writes, "at present the requisite historical experience and theoretical understanding may be lacking . . . we must advance by trial and error."[2] Even so, however, he argues that the private funding of political campaigns is not adequate to the task.

Though Rawls does not attempt to provide a blueprint by which to achieve political equality, he does indicate that "one guideline" required to achieve that goal is the need "to keep political parties independent of large concentrations of private economic and social power." To achieve that objective, Rawls writes, "society must bear at least a large part of the cost of organizing and carrying out the political process and must regulate the conduct of elections." A system of publicly financed election campaigns is necessary, according to Rawls, to ensure that "all citizens, whatever their social or economic

---

[2] John Rawles, *Political Liberalism* (New York: Columbia University Press, 1996), p. 328.

'position'" have "a fair opportunity to hold public office and to influence the outcome of political decisions."[3]

The argument presented here is fourfold. The first claim is that the current political system has failed and likely will continue to fail to provide a countervailing offset to the increasing domestic income inequality driven by technological change and globalization. The second is that it is possible for policy interventions to offset such advancing inequality. The third claim is that the kind of egalitarian politics that Rawls calls for is necessary to legislate such policies. That, in turn, requires the public financing of election campaigns. Obviously, therefore, the fourth claim is that a radical reform of the American political system is needed, one that reduces the role of private wealth in funding our political system. We need to pay for election campaigns publicly. Such a reform will occur only if a grassroots movement on its behalf creates sufficient political pressure to compel its adoption.

Structurally, this book is divided into seven chapters. In Chapter 1, I discuss how technological change and globalization have produced a strong tendency toward income inequality throughout the developed world. In Chapter 2, I examine the extent to which political processes in Europe have been successful in offsetting income inequality and contrast the

---

[3] John Rawls, *Political Liberalism* (New York: Columbia University Press, 1996), p. 327.

relatively poor performance of the United States in this regard. Chapter 3 then takes up the question of the financing of election campaigns in the United States. In it, I discuss the policy biases that result from our political system, dependent as it is upon private political contributions. Chapter 4 discusses the history of campaign funding in the United States and the recent efforts at reform. In Chapter 5, I look at the attitudes Americans have toward their government and what would be required for them to reverse their stance of mistrust and hostility toward the public sector. Chapter 6 is concerned with the extent to which the public funding of elections could advance the cause of a more egalitarian politics, and considers challenges from both the right and the left to such a reform. This serves as a prelude to the concluding discussion in Chapter 7 that explores the political work necessary to achieve a deepening of the democratic content of American politics.

1

The Economics of Income Inequality

Since 1980, income inequality has increased through-out the developed world. This pattern is reported in Table 1.1 where gini coefficients for twelve developed countries including the United States are displayed for both 1980 and 2000.[1] Between those years, income inequality grew in ten of those nations.

This table also reveals that the growth in income inequality that occurred in the United States during these years exceeded that of any of the other eleven countries, with the exception of the United Kingdom. As a result, this country, already experiencing in 1980 the dubious distinction of possessing the most unequal distribution of income, saw its status in this regard worsen over this period. Our gini coefficient of 0.368 in 2000 was one-third higher than the mean for the other eleven

[1] The gini coefficient is a frequently used measure of income inequality that is computed by estimating the extent to which low-income households receive less than their proportionate share of the national income and high-income households a greater share. The higher the coefficient, the greater the inequality.

nations. What this means is that the poor in the United States received one-third less of the national income and the rich one-third more than was the case elsewhere.

A country's distribution of income results from two distinct and separable processes: the functioning of its markets and the functioning of its political system. The market-determined distribution of income itself emerges from what happens in labor markets and what happens in financial markets. In labor markets, inequality exists among households because the wages that people receive in exchange for their labor differ according to the demand for and the supply of the varying skills they possess. This inequality is reinforced and intensified by the payment of property income in the form of interest, dividends, and rent – payments made to individuals by virtue of their owning assets such as stocks, bonds, and buildings. Because these financial assets tend to be disproportionately owned by a narrow segment of the population, the distribution of property income tends to increase the income inequality that emerges from labor markets.

Systems of taxation and social programs, adopted in the political process, alter this income configuration. Almost invariably, these programs and policies in combination increase the share of the national income that goes to poor and middle-income households and thus decreases the share that goes to the rich. In general, that is, taxes and social programs reduce income inequality. The gini coefficient is lower

The Economics of Income Inequality

Table 1.1. Changes in the gini coefficient, circa 1980–2000

Country	1980 Gini	2000 Gini	Change in Gini
United Kingdom	0.270^a	0.345^b	+0.075
United States	0.301^a	0.368	+0.067
Sweden	0.197^c	0.252	+0.055
Belgium	0.227^d	0.277	+0.050
Finland	0.209^e	0.247	+0.038
Austria	0.227^e	0.260	+0.033
Australia	0.281^c	0.311^f	+0.030
Norway	0.223^a	0.251	+0.028
Germany	0.244^c	0.264	+0.020
Canada	0.284^c	0.302	+0.018
France	0.288^c	0.288^f	0.000
Netherlands	0.260^g	0.248^b	−0.012

[a] 1979.
[b] 1999.
[c] 1981.
[d] 1985.
[e] 1987.
[f] 1994.
[g] 1983.

Source: Gary Burtless and Christopher Jencks, "American Inequality and Its Consequences" in Henry J. Aaron, James M. Lindsay, and Pietro S. Nivolo (eds.), *Agenda for the Nation* (Washington, DC: The Brookings Institution, 2003), p. 76.

when those forms of public policies are taken into account than when they are not.

In principle, the rise in inequality observed in Table 1.1 could have resulted from changes either in market or political processes. It might have been the case that equality-promoting social and economic policies remained unchanged, but the income generated in labor and financial markets became increasingly concentrated in high-income households. Alternatively, there might have been stability in the pattern of income emerging from markets, but there could have been a retreat from government policies promoting equality. And of course, it is possible that the shift to greater income inequality occurred because of changes in both. Market rewards might have become more unequal, and there might in addition have been a shift away from government policies benefiting low-income individuals.

The available evidence strongly suggests that the widespread increase in income inequality that we have observed occurred primarily because of changed market outcomes, not because of altered government policies. In a 1997 article covering most of the period of concern here, Peter Gottschalk and Timothy M. Smeeding compared the changes that occurred in the distribution of income emerging from markets (described as "market income inequality") with the changes in the distribution of income after taxes and social programs were taken into account (the "disposable income inequality"). What they were interested in observing was the extent to which the changes that occurred in one corresponded to the changes that occurred in the other. If the two were closely related – if the growth in market income inequality approximated the growth in disposable income inequality – the inference was that the latter was probably caused by the former. Overall inequality grew because of what happened in markets; government policy was not responsible. If, however, disposable income inequality grew more than market income inequality, this was taken as evidence that government policies to reduce inequality had become less effective.

What Gottschalk and Smeeding found was that in almost all of the countries included in their study, the growth in market income inequality and the growth in disposable income inequality closely tracked each other (Table 1.2). That is, in nine of the twelve countries, observed changes in the way incomes were paid in markets were similar to the changes that occurred in the incomes households received. The experience in the United States corresponds to this pattern. In this country, both market income inequality and disposable income inequality increased by about 30 percent between 1980 and 1993.

Of the three countries where there was a divergence between market income inequality and disposable income inequality, in two of them, Germany and Finland, disposable income inequality grew less than market income equality, indicating that in those countries public policy had become increasingly effective in achieving egalitarian outcomes. Only in Great Britain is there evidence of a decreased public policy commitment to reduce inequality. In that country,

Table 1.2. Change in market and disposable income inequality

Country	Years	Market income inequality	Disposable income inequality
United Kingdom	1980–93	+++	++++
United States	1980–93	+++	+++
Sweden	1980–93	+++	+++
Australia	1980–91	+	+
Netherlands	1981–9	+	+
Norway	1982–9	+	+
Belgium	1985–92	+	+
Canada	1980–92	+	0
Finland	1981–92	+++	0
France	1979–89	0	0
Germany	1983–90	+	0

$0 = -4\%$ to $+4\%$.

$+ = 5\%$ to 10%.

$++ = 11\%$ to 15%.

$+++ = 16\%$ to 29%.

$++++ = 30\%$ or more.

Source: Peter Gottschalk and Timothy M. Smeeding, "Cross-National Comparisons and Earnings and Income Inequality," *Journal of Economic Literature*, Vol. 35, No. I 2 (June 1997), Table 4, p. 666.

disposable income inequality increased more than market income inequality.

What these data suggest, therefore, is that what happened generally to the distribution of income among the developed countries occurred because of the way income was received in markets and not principally because government tax and transfer policies became less egalitarian. Changes in market processes, not a retreat from social programs, explain why income became more concentrated during these years. Economists analyzing why market incomes have become more unequal have emphasized the complexity of the process. In almost all cases, they emphasize the changes that have occurred in the labor market, trying to understand the growing divergences that have emerged among wage earners. Demographic factors such as the age structure of the population and the increased number of single-parent households play a role, as do social norms including those governing the participation of women in the labor market. The widespread decline in union representation is part of the process as well. In the United States, furthermore, the role of corporate governance is significant in light of the dramatically increased incomes of chief executive officers of corporations in this country, a phenomenon that has not occurred elsewhere.[2]

Despite these considerations, most students of the growth in inequality identify technological change as their analytic starting point. They point to two principal mechanisms by

[2] Ian Dew-Becker and Robert J. Gordon, "Where Did the Productivity Growth Go? Inflation Dynamics and the Distribution of Income," National Bureau of Economic Research, Working Paper 11842, http://www.nber.org/papers/w11842, p. 57. The possibility that executive compensation might increase in Europe in the way that has already occurred in the United States is discussed in Geraldine Fabrikant, "U.S.-Style Pay Deals for Chiefs Become All the Rage in Europe," *The New York Times*, June 16, 2006, http://www.selectnytimes.com.

which the appearance of the new technologies of communication, information processing and storage – dating from the 1980s – have resulted in an increase in market-based income inequality. The first derives from the fact that the new technologies are skill-biased. The second is that those advances have facilitated the spread of economic development to poor countries – the process of economic globalization. Both, they argue, have intensified differences in income-earning capacities in the developed world.

The skill-bias argument starts with the assumption that new technologies require more highly educated workers than earlier technologies did. But because workers with high levels of education are in relatively limited supply, this change in the demand for labor has resulted in a widening gap in labor incomes. Firms competing with each other for the services of scarce well-educated employees are forced to offer them attractive pay packages. At the same time, workers with little education and fewer skills find the demand for their services declining. As a result, their compensation falls, at least relative to the pay of those who are benefiting from the new pattern of labor demand. What emerges is a growing gap in what is paid to one group of employees compared to the other.

Implicit in this argument is the assumption that the growth in the demand for highly educated labor exceeds the growth in its supply. If that were not the case, the wage premium for high-level employees would not increase. The skill bias of technology increases inequality only if the growth in the demand for high-level labor is not matched by an increased availability of such personnel. Seen from this perspective, inequality arises just as much from an insufficient growth in the number of adequately trained and educated employees as it does from the altered skill and human capital requirements associated with the new technology.

Indeed, Gottschalk and Smeeding demonstrate precisely that. Their analysis points to the growth in the supply of highly educated workers as the key determinant of the growth in inequality caused by technological change. Where the supply of educated workers increased the most, income inequality grew the least. In this regard, Gottschalk and Smeeding cite specifically the cases of Germany, the Netherlands, and Canada, where the growth in the availability of highly educated labor was sufficient to minimize the growth in inequality. In contrast, the United States, the United Kingdom, and Sweden were countries in which the supply of workers with high levels of education grew relatively slowly. As a result, the wage premium offered to skilled workers in those countries increased and the distribution of income became more unequal.[3] In short, technological change does not inevitably produce wage inequality. It did so because countries like the

[3] Peter Gottschalk and Timothy M. Smeeding, "Cross-National Comparisons and Earnings and Income Inequality" *Journal of Economic Literature*, Vol. 35, No. 2 (June 1997), p. 655.

United States did not respond effectively to changing labor force requirements.

A variant on the argument that emphasizes changes in the domestic labor market has been offered by Edward N. Wolff. Wolff warns against the too facile assumption that the jobs created by new technologies require high levels of skill. He distinguishes between "knowledge-producing" workers and "data" workers. Wolff believes that most of the growth in the demand for labor occurring in association with the new technology in the United States was not for highly skilled professionals and managers who create knowledge, but rather for workers with only moderate skills in clerical and sales occupations. He thinks that the new technologies have produced a hollowing out of the labor force. The growth in the number of knowledge workers has been more than offset by an even greater growth in the number of limited-skill data workers, while the employment of middle-skill data workers has declined. Wolff calculates that in its net effect, computerization has resulted in a "deskilling" of the labor force.[4] With that change in employment patterns, income inequality has increased, according to Wolff. Those at the top do very well, while the rest of the information technology labor force is paid at levels consistent with their limited technical training.

[4] Edward N. Wolff, *Does Education Really Help? Skill, Work and Inequality* (New York: Oxford University Press, 2006), pp. 27, 65,157, 233.

Even Wolff's dissent, however, can be interpreted as supporting the hypothesis that the real problem causing inequality is not technological change but the way a country responds to it. If most computer-related jobs in fact are only clerical positions requiring little formal education, the fact of the growing wage premium at the top of the occupational structure suggests a shortage in the availability of the kinds of workers who can fill these positions. Increasing their supply would dampen down the growth in incomes at that level and at least reduce the growth of wage inequality. Wolff's argument too, like that of Gottschalk and Smeeding, therefore can be reinterpreted as an indictment of a nation's educational system.

The spread of economic development – globalization – has been the second source of income inequality in the developed world. China, Indonesia, Turkey, the Philippines, Pakistan, and Bangladesh have all seen their manufactured exports grow at double-digit rates in the roughly two and a half decades after 1980, and India was not far behind at 9.5 percent per year.[5] As a result of these successes in manufacturing, every one of these countries achieved a per capita economic growth rate of at least 2.1 percent per year between 1980 and 2003. The most impressive achievements in this regard occurred in China and India, the two giants in Asia. China stood apart from all

[5] Calculated from the World Trade Organization, Statistical Data Base, http://www.wto.org.

other poor countries with a phenomenally high growth rate of 8.5 percent per capita per year, a figure that implies that the country's per capita output is doubling approximately every nine years. India too experienced very rapid economic growth. Though less dependent on manufactured exports than China, India's per capita growth rate of 3.8 percent per year is very high when viewed in historical perspective.[6] At that rate, its output per person would double in less than twenty years.

Obviously, economic growth rates of these magnitudes are of enormous importance. Three-fifths of the world's population live in Asia, and the two most rapidly growing nations in the region, China and India, together contain three-eighths of the world's people and almost half of the people living in poor nations. The economic modernization of countries of that size cannot help but produce a fundamental reordering of the worldwide structure of production.

Consumers in developed countries have benefited greatly from Asia's industrial revolution. Because of it, there is greater availability of manufactured goods than otherwise would have been the case. Furthermore, both the increase in supply and the low costs of production have meant that imported goods, ranging from textiles to computers, are far less expensive for

---

[6] Average annual growth of gross domestic product per capita computed from The World Bank, *World Development Report 1991* (Washington, DC: World Bank, 1991),Tables 2 and 26, and The World Bank, *World Development Indicators 2005* (Washington, DC: World Bank, 2005), Tables 4.1 and 2.1.

consumers in a country like the United States than they would be in the absence of global production networks.[7]

But globalization, like technological change, inflicts damage as well as gain. Just as the introduction of new products or new methods of production creates new patterns of demand for labor, imports transform employment and occupational patterns. Low-cost products from a previously poor country like China put at risk the market position of firms located in the United States and thereby confront their employees with the specter of reduced wages or job loss. Even as consumption and therefore wealth increase because of international trade, specific workers and firms are faced with an often costly and wrenching need to adjust to the new circumstances.

In economic theory, technological change and increased international trade have the same effect. Resources that are no longer needed – in one case because of productivity growth and in the other because imports have taken over the market – will be redeployed in new, higher-productivity activities. New firms will find market outlets for new products and will become more profitable than the old ones. It will be possible, therefore,

[7] I am not aware of estimates of the gains associated with trade with Asia. Bradford, Grieco, and Hufbauer estimate the gains for the United States associated with all of the trade liberalization that occurred between 1947 and 2002 at $600 billion, or about $2,200 per capita. See Scott C. Bradford, Paul L. E. Grieco, and Gary Clyde Hufbauer, "The Payoff to America from Global Integration," in C. Fred Bergsten(ed.), *The United States and the World Economy* (Washington, DC: Institute for International Economics, January 2005), p. 83.

to pay workers higher wages than was possible in their old jobs.

In reality, however, the adjustment process required by either new technology or new imports is not typically as neat or seamless as is described in economic theory. For this transition to occur without substantial income losses for the workers involved, new firms must come into existence quickly, the demand for labor must be sufficiently strong to enable laid-off workers to shift from one occupation to another without delay, and the skills that those workers possess must be appropriate for the newly created occupations. If one or more of these conditions is not operative, workers will not be able immediately to secure new comparably paid jobs. Imports from low-income countries, like technological change, thus have the potential to inflict harm on specific groups of workers and firms even as they hold out the prospect of aggregate gains for the society as a whole.[8]

Opponents of globalization often cite the job-displacing consequences of that process as the reason for their hostility to global market integration. But they almost never oppose technological change. That process, after all, is the principal source of modern economic growth. But because the impacts

---

[8] See Ralph E. Gomory and William J. Baumol, *Global Trade and Conflicting National Interests* (Cambridge, MA, and London: MIT Press, 2000) for a discussion of the circumstances in which these gains will not be realized.

of technological change and international trade are so similar, it is neither desirable nor even feasible to separate the victims of one from the victims of the other and offer assistance to one group but not its counterpart. Thus, there is no reason, based on their respective labor market impacts, to oppose one – globalization – while accepting the other – technological change. Justice requires that compensation be provided when workers encountering either one, experience job losses.

Indeed, Klein, Schuh, and Triest write that "in practice, it is often impossible to determine whether job displacement is due to international trade, technological change, shifts in intranational [sic] comparative advantage, changes in consumer tastes, mistakes by an establishment's or firm's management, or some other factor."[9] Furthermore, since both the positive effects and negative consequences of trade-related job losses and job losses due to technological change are so similar, it is hard to make the case that one group of workers should be provided with assistance but not the other. For that reason, most analysts agree with Lori G. Kletzer that the reason an individual loses his or her job is less important than how to help such an individual secure a new one. As she puts it, "why the job

---

[9] Michael W. Klein, Scott Schuh, and Robert K. Triest, *Job Creation, Job Destruction and International Competition* (Kalamazoo, MI: W. E. Upjohn Institute for Employment Research, 2003), p. 157.

was lost does not matter much at all." Since the characteristics of workers who are put at a loss and the consequences of their losses are similar, "policymakers should consider adjustment policy for all displaced workers and broaden program eligibility beyond 'trade-displaced workers.'"[10]

Kletzer has nevertheless attempted to identify the differences between workers who lose their jobs because of increased international trade and those who lose them for other reasons. To do so, she compiled a list of industries that she describes as "import-competing." In her definition, these are industries in which, during the 1979–94 period, imports substantially increased as a share of consumption. She then compared job displacement in these industries with job displacement in other industries in the American economy. Where statistically significant differences appeared, Kletzer attributed them to the consequence of competing against imports from abroad.[11]

Where Kletzer did find differences between the two groups of displaced workers, those differences were not profound:

1. There were virtually no differences between the two categories of workers with regard to educational attainment or job tenure.

[10] Lori G. Kletzer, *Job Loss from Imports: Measuring the Costs* (Washington, DC: Institute for International Economics , 2001), p. 6.

[11] Kletzer does not attempt to identify the consequences of job loss due to imports from specific countries or groups of countries.

2. Import-competing displaced workers were slightly less likely to find new work. At the date of the surveys on which Kletzer's analysis is based 63.4 percent of import-industry displaced workers had been reemployed compared to 65.8 percent in the other manufacturing sectors.

3. In both categories earnings losses were, in Kletzer's words, "sizable" – averaging 13 percent – and again in both were most severe for the workers with the longest tenure in their positions.[12]

What Kletzer's analysis demonstrates is the seriousness of the problems created by a dynamic economy. Workers displaced either because of technological change or because the United States is an increased participant in international trade pay a price, a penalty that in the name of equity and fairness requires a meaningful and effective political response.

What makes this situation particularly pressing is that the experience of export-oriented industrialization in Asia will certainly be replicated elsewhere. It is very likely that the large countries of Latin America, such as Brazil and Mexico, will, in the not too distant future, join China and India in experiencing rapid economic growth. When that happens, dislocations

---

[12] Kletzer, *Job Loss from Imports*, pp. 3–5.

similar to those that occurred with the economic development of Asia's giants will be repeated. Poverty in Latin America will decline and the United States in the aggregate will benefit, but the process will impose damaging dislocations on specific segments of the U.S. economy and workforce. When that occurs, implementing policies that provide assistance to the innocent victims of progress will once again become a matter of justice.

In this regard, the warning issued by Alan S. Blinder, a former vice chairman of the board of governors of the Federal Reserve, is particularly important. Blinder notes that to date, the pressures experienced by workers in the developed world as a result of the spread of economic development have been felt largely by employees in manufacturing industries. In the future, however, he anticipates that labor market competition will spread to service workers as well. As he puts it, "we have so far barely seen the tip of the offshoring iceberg, the eventual dimensions of which may be staggering."[13]

In sum, the spread of new technologies in recent years has been at the root of the nearly universal growth in income inequality that has occurred in the developed world. Changes in technology have abruptly increased the demand for high-level workers, reduced the demand for those with education levels that in the past were considered adequate for securing

---

[13] Alan S. Blinder, "Offshoring: The Next Industrial Revolution?" *Foreign Affairs*, Vol. 85, No. 2 (March–April 2006), p. 114.

well-paid jobs, and thrown many U.S. workers into competition with low-wage workers in poor nations. The fact that the supply of highly educated workers did not increase rapidly enough to match the demand, and the pressures felt in the labor market because of the enhanced productive capacity of Asian giants such as China and India, have resulted in differentiated experiences in the American labor markets. Those whose skills were scarce but greatly in demand did well; the others suffered.

The United States is a society that already possesses huge income disparities. Technological change and globalization threaten the country with an intensification of its already deep fissures. Whether that happens will be determined by the political process through which market-generated inequality can be offset. It is to the political arena that we turn next.

2

The Politics of Inequality

The fact that nearly all the developed countries have experienced growing income inequality since about 1980 suggests that their responses to the changing requirements of technology and globalization have been inadequate. Increased domestic income disparities reflect the failure to adjust sufficiently to new circumstances. Educational and training programs have not kept up with changes in the labor market.

The problem here is that it is not possible to anticipate the knowledge that new technologies require before those technologies appear. Similarly, it is all but impossible to know in advance the skill requirements of the industries that could absorb the workers displaced by globalization. As a result, education and training programs must always play catch-up. The people who develop curriculums must first understand the changed pattern of labor demand. Only then can they retool in order to provide workers with the skills that are in increased demand in the labor market. Even so, it takes time for an adequate supply of newly educated workers to make their presence felt. For these reasons, even under the best circumstances, rapid technological change can be expected to induce growing income inequality. Thus, it falls to the political process to provide counterweights to the growth in income disparities that are all too likely to appear in labor markets during periods of rapid technological change.

Such counterweights can take a variety of forms. But there are two elements that must be present if the increases in inequality are to be held in check: (1) income support must be provided to displaced workers and (2) a bridge must be constructed to facilitate the movement of displaced workers to new, well-paid jobs.

It is possible to measure the degree of success countries have achieved in this regard. The same measures used in Chapter 1 to assess the sources of growing income inequality – the gini coefficients for market income inequality and disposable income inequality – can also be used to examine the effectiveness of government efforts to offset inequality. While in the previous chapter these measures were assessed over time, in this chapter a cross-sectional analysis is undertaken in order to compare countries. Here we look at the difference between the market gini and the disposable income gini for each country as an indicator of the extent to which its government succeeded in countering the income inequality that emerged from markets. To the extent that the disposable income gini is less than

Table 2.1. Market-determined gini coefficient, disposable income gini coefficient, and percentage difference between market and disposable income gini coefficients (1990s)[a]

	Market income inequality	Disposable income inequality	Percent difference
United States	.48	.37	22.9
Canada	.42	.29	31.0
Australia	.45	.31	31.1
Norway	.40	.24	40.0
United Kingdom	.57	.34	40.4
Netherlands	.42	.25	40.5
France	.49	.29	40.8
Finland	.39	.23	41.0
Germany	.49	.26	46.9
Belgium	.50	.26	48.0
Sweden	.47	.22	53.2
Austria	NA	.28	NA
Mean for All Countries Excluding the US	.46	.27	41.3

[a] Excluding Austria.

Source: Gary Burtless and Christopher Jencks, "American Inequality and Its Consequences," in Henry J. Aaron, James M. Lindsay, and Pietro S. Nivolo (eds.), Agenda for the Nation (Washington, DC: The Brookings Institution, 2003), p. 76.

the market gini, the government is given credit for success in achieving a more egalitarian outcome than would have been the case in the absence of its intervention.

In Table 2.1 the gini coefficients for both market income inequality and disposable income inequality are presented, as is the percentage difference between them, for the same twelve countries discussed in Chapter 1. Each country observation is for a year during the 1990s. Nations are ranked according to their success in reducing market inequality, that is, by the percentage by which the disposable income gini coefficient is lower than the market gini coefficient.

What the table makes clear is that the extent to which countries offset market inequality varies greatly. At one extreme is Sweden, where the disposable income gini is less than one-half of its market gini. In Sweden, that is, taxation and income redistribution programs reduced income inequality by more than 50 percent. At the other extreme is the United States, where the difference between the two is slightly less than 23 percent. In reducing income inequality by only about one-fourth, this country did politically the least in offsetting the inequality that emerges from markets. The political processes in eight of the other eleven countries reduced income inequality by at least 40 percent, with the mean for all countries, excluding the United States, standing at 41.3 percent. The conclusion that emerges from this table is that the distribution of income produced by markets in the U.S. economy is roughly similar to that of the comparison countries. However, our political process fails to narrow the resulting income differences nearly as much as occurs elsewhere.

The data in Table 2.2 provide insight into why the United States so lags in this regard. That table ranks countries

Table 2.2. Ranking of countries by percent of GDP spent on net direct
public social expenditures and index of income tax progressivity

Country	Direct public social expenditures	Country	Index of tax progressivity[a]
France	28.2	Netherlands	5.81
Sweden	28.0	UK	1.82
Germany	26.8	Sweden	1.78
Belgium	23.6	Austria	1.69
Austria	23.5	France	1.63
UK	22.9	Germany	1.61
Norway	22.2	United States	1.59
Finland	21.7	Canada	1.50
Netherlands	19.5	Norway	1.48
Australia	19.1	Australia	1.37
Canada	18.8	Finland	1.32
United States	14.7	Belgium	1.19
Mean Excluding United States	23.1		1.93

[a] Ratio of the marginal personal income tax rate for individuals earning 167% of the average wage to that of individuals earning 67% of the average wage for central and subcentral governments.

Source: Index of Tax Progressivity: OECD Taxation of Wage Income (2000), http://www. oecd.org/dataoecd/43/46/1942474.xls; Net Direct Public Social Spending as Percent GDP, in Willem Adema and Maxime Ladaique, "Net Social Expenditures 2005 Edition" More Comprehensive Measures of Social Support (Paris: OECD, 2005), Table 6.

according to the degree to which they possess a progressive taxation system (taxing high-income households proportionately more than low-income households). It also ranks these countries according to the percentage of their gross domestic product that they spend on public social expenditures, programs that involve cash benefits (pensions, maternity payments, and social assistance), social services (child care, care for the elderly and disabled), and tax breaks with a social purpose (favorable tax treatment for health care).[1]

This table reveals that what makes the United States substantially different from the other countries is its level of public social expenditures, not its tax system. The United States ranks last in the share of its gross domestic product spent on public social programs. That share is less than two-thirds of the mean for the other countries. In contrast, the degree to which the United States possesses a progressive tax system places it in the middle of the pack. With an index of tax progressivity of 1.59, the United States ranks seventh out of the twelve countries included in the table. It is true that this country's index of tax progressivity lies substantially below the mean for all of these countries. However, if the Netherlands, a country where the tax system is much more progressive than elsewhere, were excluded, the United States would possess a higher index of progressivity than the average for the other nations.

Simply put, disposable income is more unequally distributed in the United States than in the other countries because its public sector does much less to promote equality.

---

[1] Willem Adema and Maxime Ladaique, "Net Social Expenditure, 2005 Edition," *OECD Social, Employment and Migration Working Papers No. 29* (Paris: OECD), p. 7.

The Politics of Inequality

The European political system is more responsive to the interests of those at the low end of the income distribution. Christopher Jencks is right when, in answer to his own question of why income distribution in the United States is more unequal than elsewhere, he responds that "legislators [in the United States] have... shown a persistent preference for relying on private markets rather than public institutions to make economic decisions."[2]

This negative assessment receives confirmation in data compiled by the Organization for Economic Cooperation and Development (OECD). Among the developed countries, the United States ranks at or near the bottom in each of four categories of worker support when expenditures are expressed as a percentage of gross domestic product (see Table 2.3). Unlike most of these nations, the United States provides no early retirement support, ranks at the bottom (tied with Norway) in providing funds for subsidized employment, and is next to the bottom in making funds available for retraining. Overall, only the United Kingdom and Norway spend less as a share of their economic output on active labor market programs. Indeed, eight of these fifteen countries spend proportionately twice as much as the United States does on these programs.

[2] Christopher Jencks, "Why Do So Many Jobs Pay So Badly?" in James Lardner and David A. Smith (eds.), *Inequality Matters* (New York: New Press, 2005), pp. 134, 135.

Table 2.3. Labor market programs as a percentage of GDP

	Training	Subsidized employment	Unempl. comp.	Early retirement	Total
United Kingdom	0.02	0.03	0.37	0	0.42
Norway	0.05	0.01	0.54	0	0.60
United States	0.03	0.01	0.57	0	0.61
Canada	0.15	0.03	0.80	0	0.98
Italy	0.05	0.32	0.54	0.10	1.01
Switzerland	0.13	0.13	0.77	0	1.03
Australia	0.03	0.10	1.00	na	1.13
Sweden	0.29	0.21	1.04	0.01	1.55
Austria	0.21	0.10	1.12	0.13	1.56
France	0.23	0.35	1.63	0.17	2.38
Netherlands	0.60	0.33	1.72	0	2.65
Germany	0.32	0.22	2.10	0.03	2.67
Finland	0.30	0.33	1.53	0.53	2.69
Belgium	0.30	0.60	1.94	0.45	3.29
Denmark	0.86	0.17	1.37	1.87	4.27

Source: Computed from OECD *Employment Outlook, 2005*; Statistical Annex, Table H.

Though it is true that the United States generally does not engage in as much public spending to offset the inequalities that emerge from its markets as other countries do, the fact remains that in some cases the United States uses programs that have not been employed elsewhere. Alone among the developed countries, the United States has adopted a specific set of policies to help workers displaced by increased imports. Its Trade Adjustment Assistance (TAA) program was first adopted in 1962. Since then, it has been amended several times, most recently in 2002. In addition, a similar program was implemented with the adoption of the North American Free Trade Agreement (NAFTA).

Unhappily, however, these programs have been administered with a studied indifference by the Department of Labor. Furthermore, they are seriously weakened by the fact that employees who work in service industries (upward of 80 percent of the labor force), as opposed to those who work in manufacturing sectors, have been ruled ineligible to receive benefits.[3] These and other weaknesses, write Lori G. Kletzer and Howard Rosen, "give rise to questions about America's fundamental commitment to assisting all workers adversely affected by changes in international trade and investment.... [4]

According to Kletzer and Rosen, "only a minority of workers are eligible for and receive U[employment] I[nsurance] when they lose their jobs," and even when they are eligible, the level of assistance that they receive is "low." Funding for job training and job search programs is limited. Kletzer and Rosen report that "very few workers received meaningful training."[5] What all

---

[3] Erika Kinetz, "Trading Down: The U.S. Shortchanges Its Outsourced Workers," *Harper's Magazine*, July 2005, pp. 62–4.

[4] Lori G. Kletzer and Howard Rosen, "Easing the Adjustment Burden on U.S. Workers," in C. Fred Bergsten (ed.), *The United States and the World Economy* (Washington, D.C.: Institute for International Economics, January 2005), p. 332.

[5] Ibid., pp. 314, 315.

of this suggests is that the TAA is of very limited use in offsetting the problems caused for individual workers by globalization. The U.S. pattern is clear. We spend far less to redress the inequalities that emanate from market processes than other countries, and we are far less committed to counter the negative consequences of technological change and globalization. The result of this parsimony is that the income inequalities in this country are stark compared to those of other countries. Furthermore, in this era of globalization, only weak counterweights stand in the way of a deepening of the inequalities that already mar this country.

Government inaction has meant that more people than necessary have been injured by the twin processes of technological change and economic globalization. J. David Richardson puts it this way: With modern globalization, "American workers, firms, and communities with high skills, mobility and global engagement have prospered handsomely. Those with average skills, low mobility and little capability for global engagement have enjoyed disproportionally [sic] few gains."[6]

This uneven pattern of benefits and costs could and should have been made more egalitarian. It is simply not fair that those sections of the population already well endowed with human capital should see their privileged status enhanced by

---

[6] J. David Richardson, "Uneven Gains and Unbalanced Burdens? Three Decades of American Globalization," in Bergsten (ed.), *The United States and the World Economy*, pp. 115, 111.

globalization, while the relative position of others who possess less human capital declines.

Few observers believe that the United States in the future will adopt the policies necessary to reduce the burdens of technological change and globalization on its victims. Kletzer and Rosen stand for the consensus. They write that despite the need to strengthen labor market adjustment programs, "both Democratic and Republican policymakers have not shown any political will in pursuing such needed reform."[7] The reason for this is clear. As I. M. Destler and Peter J. Balint's study of trade policy put it, "the trade policymaking system in Washington centers on producer interests. It is managed by governmental institutions (e.g., USTR, the congressional trade committees) oriented toward these interests, adept at balancing them and possessing credibility with them." Worker's needs and interests are neglected, they go on, because addressing those concerns would "invite clashes along ideological lines.... " Rather than put at risk the business coalition that promotes international trade and investment liberalization, "the trade policy community and its export-oriented business allies have been wary of bringing these issues on board."[8]

---

[7] Kletzer and Rosen, "Easing the Adjustment Burden on U.S. Workers," p. 331.

[8] I. M. Destler and Peter J. Balint, *The New Politics of American Trade: Trade, Labor and the Environment* (Washington, DC: Institute for International Economics, 1999), p. 46.

This is the context that provides meaning to Lester C. Thurow's argument that "unless compensation is actually paid, the losers are not being economically illiterate when they exercise their democratic right to oppose free trade in a democracy." As he points out, "democracy does not demand that its voters be philosopher kings, worried about the general welfare but uninterested in their own personal welfare." Thurow is particularly incensed that the economics profession has failed to stress the need to provide compensation to the victims of progress while emphasizing the virtues of free trade. He writes that, "in practice the economics profession defends free trade even when it knows that the winners will not be compensating the losers. And in fact compensation is almost never paid."[9]

Survey data indicate that the American people are responding to globalization in precisely the way that Thurow suggests. According to Kenneth F. Scheve and Matthew J. Slaughter, "a wide range of public opinion surveys report that a plurality or a majority of U.S. citizens oppose policies to further liberalize trade, immigration and FDI [foreign direct investment]." This opposition exists despite the fact that a majority does acknowledge the existence of gains from international trade such as greater product variety, lower import prices, and increased

---

[9] Lester C. Thurow, "Do Only Economic Illiterates Argue That Trade Can Destroy Jobs and Lower America's National Income?" *Social Research*, Vol. 71, No. 2 (Summer 2004), p. 270.

product-market competition for producers. But what worries Americans are the resulting "adverse labor market impacts," and they weigh these more heavily than the benefits. In particular, this opposition to globalization is strongly related to labor market skills. As Scheve and Slaughter put it, "less skilled individuals, measured by educational attainment or wages earned, are much more likely to oppose freer trade and immigration than their more skilled counterparts." For workers with relatively limited skills, "globalization is perceived to be an important source of wage pressure," and for that reason it is opposed.[10]

Particularly in the context of the limited labor market and income support provided to low-wage workers in this country, these findings come as no surprise. As we have seen, technological change and globalization do create innocent victims, and these victims are disproportionately people with limited skills. For them to do anything but oppose these contemporary forms of economic modernization, as they currently are implemented, would be irrational. These economic advances do put them at risk, and they resist that victimization. In this, they primarily oppose globalization. That process is seen as more likely to be reversed than technological change. As Scheve and Slaughter point out, most people believe that technological

---

[10] Kenneth F. Scheve and Matthew J. Slaughter, *Globalization and the Perceptions of American Workers* (Washington, DC: Institute for International Economics, 2001), pp. 9, 11.

change is inexorable but that globalization can be slowed or reversed with appropriate policies.[11] Thus, while a Luddite-type opposition to technological change possesses no political traction, there is a strong antiglobalization political constituency among the American people.

The problem here, however, is that opposition to globalization represents no less a dangerous blind alley than would resistance to technological advance. It is very unlikely that the spread of economic development globally will or can be reversed. It is hard to believe, for example, that China, India, or any of the other Asian countries that have experienced recent economic growth will in the foreseeable future reverse the policies that have generated their successes. Much more likely is the spread of economic growth to other currently poor nations. If this conjecture is true, it will be increasingly difficult and costly for the United States to stand in opposition. For the fact is that with the spread of economic modernization, the potential gains from trade to American consumers increase.

Furthermore, there are great dangers associated with a retreat to protectionism and nationalism over and above the economic costs that would be incurred. The domestic political dynamic that might well be triggered if the country resolutely turns inward could be fearsome. A powerful xenophobia might be created, an attitude of hostility to things foreign

---

[11]   Ibid., p. 11.

that could result in scapegoating at home (particularly of the large and growing immigrant population) and, if allowed to go unchecked, even result in dangerous military adventures overseas.

The country need not go in this direction. It is possible to reduce the burdens that workers experience in this period of rapid economic change. Indeed, the survey data used by Scheve and Slaughter point to the very policies that might enlist support for globalization or at least mitigate opposition to it. It is true that, overwhelmingly, respondents in the United States believe that job retraining efforts in this country are inadequate, and that in formulating U.S. trade policy, too much attention is paid to multinational corporations and too little is paid to working Americans and the general American public. Nevertheless, when a question concerning trade liberalization is linked with government adjustment policies, a surprisingly strong consensus emerges in favor of globalization. Given three choices – free trade with the government implementing "programs to help workers who lose their jobs," free trade without such programs, or outright opposition to free trade – 66.3 percent of respondents favor the first option, with support for the other two options nearly equal to each other.[12] The inference to be drawn seems clear. If the risks associated with globalization were ameliorated with the kinds

[12] Ibid., pp. 94–5.

41

of supportive policies that have been extensively adopted elsewhere but neglected in this country, opposition in the United States to global economic integration would likely be sharply reduced. In the next chapter, we turn to the question of why the supportive policies that would make globalization more palatable to the American people have not been adopted nor even seriously considered.

3

The Funding and Bias of American Politics

As we have seen, the U.S. income distribution is markedly more unequal than that of comparable European countries, and that inequality during the past twenty-five years has increased more in this country than anywhere else except the United Kingdom. Our country's poor performance in this regard did not occur because the pattern of rewards that emerges from markets is markedly different from that of the rest of the developed world. What fundamentally sets the American experience apart is the degree to which government spending policies offset the inequalities that emerge from markets. The political process in the United States does far less than that of other countries to counteract inequality. In this regard it is particularly noticeable that the United States lags behind other countries in developing programs to assist workers dislocated by globalization and/or technological change.

Despite this, there has been very little discussion in the United States about how to reverse the trend toward increasing inequality. It is as if, as Bill Moyers has put it, *"equality* and *inequality* are words that have been all but expunged from the political vocabulary."[1] Why is that?

One possibility is that that this political failure simply reflects the preferences of the electorate. It might be that there is a powerful popular consensus in the country that believes that redistributive policies are wrong in principle and should be eschewed. If that is the case, our uneven income distribution would reflect the democratic will of the people.

Indeed, in addressing the reasons for the weak U.S. welfare state, Albert Alesina, Edward Glaeser, and Bruce Sacerdote argue precisely this case. Their claim is that the American people do not support income transfers because they believe that the poor are undeserving of support. This antipathy, they believe, is compounded by the fact that African Americans disproportionately are the recipients of such assistance and are the objects of majority white population racism. As they put it, "... hostility between the races limits support for welfare" and "it is clear that racial heterogeneity within the US is one of the most important reasons why the welfare state in America is small."[2]

---

[1] Bill Moyers, "The Fight of Our Lives," in James Lardner and David A. Smith (eds.), *Inequality Matters: The Growing Economic Divide in America and Its Poisonous Consequences* (New York: New Press, 2005), p. 3 (emphasis in the original).

[2] Alberto Alesina, Edward Glaeser, and Bruce Sacerdote, "Why Doesn't the U.S. Have a European-Style Welfare State?" Harvard Institute of Economic Research, Discussion Paper Number 1933 (Cambridge, MA: Harvard University, November 2001), p. 33.

To be sure, Alesina et al. do cite impediments to redistributive schemes caused by the structure of government in the United States. They find, for example, that nations with systems of proportional representation, unlike the winner-take-all system in the United States, are more likely to have large government transfer programs. But more generally, they think that attitudes in the United States simply are different than those elsewhere. They doubt that "a change in the electoral rules for Congress would have turned the United States welfare state into one like those of France or Sweden."[3] Though these authors do not formally commit themselves to an explanation in which negative attitudes toward the welfare state are the primary explanation of its weakness in the United States, the logic of their presentation points in that direction. What this, in turn, boils down to is the fact that the poor in the United States are viewed with disdain and that programs to support them are viewed with hostility by the wider public.

Serious questions can, however, be raised concerning the power of this analysis. Those doubts emerge in particular from the survey question Alesina et al. relied on in coming to their conclusion. In using the General Social Survey (GSS) data, the authors focused on the question "Do you think that the state should spend more on welfare?" The formulation of this question almost certainly biased the outcome that was obtained.

[3] Ibid., pp. 28, 2, 23.

45

In American political discourse, "welfare" specifically refers to a program created during the Depression entitled Aid to Families with Dependent Children (AFDC). The longevity of the program and the changes in family structures that occurred during the almost fifty years of its existence made it an easy target for critics by the 1990s. Because the program by then was being implemented in far different circumstances and with very different expectations with respect to marriage, divorce, and female labor force participation than when it was first implemented, AFDC increasingly came to be perceived as producing perverse incentives and outcomes. By the 1990s, if not earlier, it had become thoroughly stigmatized.

Because welfare had almost universally come to be seen negatively, it was phased out at the national level by the Clinton administration. There are strong seasons to believe, therefore, that the emotional baggage associated with the term welfare evoked a different response than would have resulted if a more neutral formulation had been used.

In fact, since 1972 the GSS has asked a different question, one that probably is less influenced by the stigma associated with welfare and that therefore may more accurately reveal what Americans think about redistributive programs. This question asked whether respondents believe that the government should reduce income differences between the rich and the poor. In the question, it was suggested that this might

Table 3.1. Survey data response to the question of whether the government should reduce income differences

	Favorable	Neutral	Opposed	Total
1972–2004				
All	46.4	20.2	33.3	99.9
Male	43.0	18.5	38.5	100.0
Female	49.4	21.6	29.1	100.1
By decade				
1970s	47.9	21.0	31.0	99.9
1980s	48.1	19.6	32.3	100.0
1990s	45.1	21.0	34.0	100.1
2000s	45.3	19.9	34.9	100.1

Source: General Social Survey, Quick Table: GSS 1972–2004 Cumulative Data File, http://sda.berkeley.edu:8080/quicktables/quickoptions.do.

be done by raising the taxes of wealthy families or by giving income assistance to the poor. Respondents were asked to state where they stood on a scale ranging from 1 (meaning that government should act to reduce income differences) to 7 (meaning that government should not concern itself with reducing income differences). By avoiding the term welfare, this question minimized the negative connotations associated with it.

Table 3.1 reports on the responses to this question by grouping together those who answered 1, 2 or 3, and describing them as favorable toward redistributive programs. Those who replied 5, 6 or 7 were judged to be opposed and those who answered 4 were considered neutral.

The data demonstrate a clear pattern. Throughout the entire period during which this question was asked, a remarkably stable plurality responded that the government should act to reduce income disparities. Almost one-half of those questioned during this thirty-two-year period favored such programs, while one-third opposed them. Women supported them more than did men, but even among the latter, those in favor exceeded those opposed. There was a slight erosion in support over time. The peak favorable score was recorded in the 1980s, when 48.1 percent of respondents answered in support. But after a decline of three percentage points during the 1990s, the percentage in favor stabilized after 2000.

It is obvious that the almost complete absence of political debate about the country's distribution of income is not attributable to an implacable hostility to income transfer programs on the part of the American people. Together, those who responded in favor of government's acting to achieve greater equality and those who declared themselves to be neutral on the subject represented two-thirds of the sample. It certainly is reasonable to suggest that something close to that percentage would at least welcome an open debate on the subject. To be sure, we cannot know where, after such a debate, the neutrals would fall. But the fact remains that no such debate is publicly underway or promises to be in the near future. This void does not reflect the preferences of the majority of the electorate. Why, then, is the increasingly unequal income redistribution not on the political agenda? Why is the United States so different from other comparable countries in its response to economic dislocations? What explains the fact that, when polled, the public expresses support for redistributive policies but the political process itself exhibits almost no expression of those preferences?

The answers to these questions lie in the structure of American politics. Since the attitudes of Americans toward income transfers are not unremittingly hostile, the weaknesses of our policies in this regard must lie in our political process. We do so little to offset income inequality because of the way we construct our political agenda.

The fact is that the United States is not only an outlier in its support for displaced workers, it is also alone in how it pays for its political campaigns. As indicated in Table 3.2, only the United States provides no public funding for political parties or candidates for its national legislature. Since the mid-1970s there has existed a voluntary system of public support for presidential candidates.[4] However, the failure to fund the

---

[4] A major problem with the presidential election system is that it was not indexed to the inflation rate. The real value of the public funds available to candidates therefore has declined with the passage of time. See Peter Overby, "Big Campaigns Undermine Public-Financing System," NPR, February 24, 2007. http://www.npr.org.

Table 3.2. Public funding of national election

	Not Earmarked	Party administration	Election campaign activities	Other	Free media access
United States	No	No	No	No	No
Australia	Yes	No	No	No	No
Austria	No	Yes	Yes	No	No
Belgium	Yes	No	No	No	Yes
Canada	No	No	Yes	No	Yes
Finland	Yes	Yes	No	No	No
France	No	Yes	Yes	No	Yes
Germany	Yes	No	No	No	Yes
Netherlands	No	No	No	Yes	Yes
Norway	Yes	Yes	No	No	Yes
Sweden	Yes	Yes	No	No	Yes
United Kingdom	No	Yes	No	No	Yes

Source: International Institute for Democracy and Electoral Assisstance, "Direct Public Funding" and "Indirect Public Funding: Media Access," at http://www.idea.int/parties/finance/db/comparison_view.cfm.

presidential public financing system adequately has resulted in its becoming largely inoperative. Serious candidates, able to raise larger sums outside of the system, have chosen not to participate in it.[5] The United States is also the only country,

[5] As reported in *The New York Times,* "... the 2008 presidential election is widely expected to be the first campaign since President Richard M. Nixon left office that would be paid for mainly by private donors and waged

aside from Finland and Australia, in which free media access is not offered to office seekers. The specifics of public funding schemes elsewhere vary, and in no case have private donations been eliminated altogether. Nevertheless, the absence of any public funding for elections to the U.S. Congress sets off the American system from the rest.

According to Karl-Heinz Nassmacher, until the 1950s the use of taxpayers' money to support political parties in developed countries "was virtually unknown." Since then, he writes, there has been a "dramatic spread of public subsidies to parties," and "today public subsidies seem to be a necessity."[6] Marcin Walecki, another authority on the subject, agrees, maintaining that "public subsidies for political parties have already become a dominating feature of most democracies."[7] According to Nassmacher, the public funding systems used in Europe are sufficiently large to cover "most of the cost of operating party headquarters on a permanent basis."[8]

without legal spending limits ... [because the public system] cannot keep up with the flow of private contributions available to the candidates." David K. Kirkpatrick, "Obama Proposes Candidates Limit General Election Spending," *The New York Times*, February 8, 2007, http://nytimes.com.

[6] Karl-Heinz Nassmacher, "Comparative Political Finance in Established Democracies," in Karl-Heinz Nassmacher (ed.), *Foundations for Democracy: Approaches to Comparative Political Finance* (Baden-Baden: Nomos Verlagsgesellschaft, 2001), p. 10.

[7] Marcin Walecki "Political Finance in Central Eastern Europe," in ibid., p. 401.

[8] Nassmacher, "Comparative Political Finance," p. 16.

Thus, the United States stands alone among the developed countries both in providing no public support for candidates or their parties in campaigns for the U.S. Congress and in providing no candidates with subsidized access to the mass media. Congressional office seekers in the United States, unlike in the rest of the developed world, are entirely dependent on their ability to raise funds from private sources. As a result, more than elsewhere, the funding of political campaigns in the United States is all but monopolized by wealthy donors.

A survey of political participation published in 1995 by Sidney Verba, Kay Lehman Schlozman, and Henry E. Brady reveals that high-income people overwhelmingly provide the resources politicians need to run their campaigns and to attain elected office. As reported in Table 3.3, their survey revealed that a tiny fraction of the population, the wealthiest 3 percent, provided more than one-third (35 percent) of the contributions to office seekers. Furthermore, the wealthiest 9 percent of the population was responsible for more than half (55 percent) of the donations. The limited role of the poor and the middle class in providing money to the political system is also stark. The poorest one-fifth (19 percent) of the sample were, as the authors put it, "barely visible" in this regard, providing 2 percent of the contributions. Indeed three-quarters of the population (74 percent) provided only about one-fourth (28 percent) of the political contributions. As Verba et al. put it, "the special inequality associated with monetary contributions affects the

Table 3.3. Population sample ranked by level of income
and percent of political donations

Level of income	Percent of population	Percent of campaign contributions
Above $125,000	3	35
$75,000–124,999	6	20
$50,000–74,999	16	18
$35,000–49,999	21	12
$15,000–34,999	36	14
Under $14,999	19	2

Source: Sidney Verba, Kay Lehman Schlozman, and Henry E. Brady, *Voice and Equality: Civic Voluntarism in American Politics* (Cambridge, MA, and London: Harvard University Press, 1995), Fig. 7.4, p. 194.

poor most strongly, but it also means that most of the middle class is underrepresented as well."[9]

These findings are corroborated in a similar survey undertaken by Peter L. Francia and his associates. After reviewing the data they had collected, these authors wrote, "if the donor pool looked like America, one might not care that a small number of donors provide so much of the funding for congressional candidates. But the donor pool clearly looks like an 'upper-class choir.' Contributors to House and Senate campaigns are overwhelmingly rich and well-educated, and they are also

[9] Sidney Verba, Kay Lehman Schlozman, and Henry E. Brady, *Voice and Equality: Civic Voluntarism in American Politics* (Cambridge, MA, and London: Harvard University Press, 1995), pp. 193, 195.

Table 3.4. Occupational structure of political donors
and the U.S. labor force

Occupation	Donors	Labor force
Business executive	52	10
Attorney	17	1
Medical professions	13	5
Education and media	11	7

Source: Peter L. Francia, John C. Green, Paul S. Herrnson, Lynda W. Powell, and Clyde Wilcox, *The Financiers of Congressional Elections: Investors, Ideologues and Intimates* (New York: Columbia University Press, 2003), Table 2.4, p. 28; labor force data computed from *Statistical Abstract of the United States 2004–2005* (Washington, DC: Government Printing Office, 2005), Table 597.

overwhelmingly middle-aged white men."[10] As a group, politi-cal donors are also very different from the rest of the population with regard to how they make a living.

Table 3.4 reports on the occupations of the people in the survey who made donations and compares that distribution to the occupations of the American labor force as a whole. The contrasts are striking. Though business executives constitute only about 10 percent of the labor force, they represented more than one-half (52 percent) of political donors. Similar dispro-portions are present for lawyers, medical professionals, and educators. As Francia et al. note, "disparities in income and

[10] Peter L. Francia, John C. Green, Paul S. Herrnson, Lynda W. Powell, and Clyde Wilcox, *The Financiers of Congressional Elections* (New York: Columbia University Press, 2003), p. 27.

education are reflected in the occupations of donors and everyday citizens. Overall businessmen and professionals dominate the donor pool."[11]

Data compiled by the Center for Responsive Politics (CRP) make it very clear that individuals associated with the U.S. business community are largely the people who fund the American political system (Table 3.5). The CRP uses four categories in grouping the funds provided to candidates, to parties, and to political action committees (PACs). These funds are provided by individuals associated with (1) businesses, (2) unions, (3) ideological and single-issue organizations, or (4) miscellaneous groups.[12] About 80 percent of the private funds donated during the 2003–4 electoral cycle were categorized this way. Using these data, it is possible to determine how much money individual donors in each category provided to the election campaigns, as well as how these funds

[11] Ibid.

[12] The ideological sector, in the CRP's words, includes "groups as diverse as the National Rifle Association, the Sierra Club and EMILY's List." In recent years, it goes on, "the most generous donors by far in this sector have been organized by current and former officeholders at the federal and state level. The sector includes groups active in debates over abortion, the environment, foreign policy, gun policy, human rights (including gay rights), Israel policy and women's issues." The "Other" sector includes "educators, government employees (though not their unions), non-profits and religious groups" With regard to the "Other" category "the biggest dollars, by far, come from the large and diverse group of donors listing their occupation as 'retired.'" see http://www.opensecrets.org/background.asp?Ind=W&cycle=2006 and http://www.opensecrets.org/background.asp?Ind=Q&cycle=2006.

Table 3.5. Individual contributions to candidates, parties, and PACs by sector and party, 2004 electoral cycle ($000s)

	Democrats		Republicans		Both parties	
	Amount	Percent of total	Amount	Percent of total	Amount	Percent of total
Business	401,678	47	613,021	70	1,014,699	59
Lawyers/lobbyists	149,844	17	60,111	7	209,955	12
Labor	53,662	6	7,711	1	61,373	4
Single-issue and ideological	111,103	13	68,693	8	179,796	10
Other	141,420	17	121,581	14	263,001	15
Total	857,707	100	871,117	100	1,728,824	100

Source: Computed from The Center for Responsive Politics, "The Big Picture 2004 Cycle, Total By Sector," http://www.opensecrets.org/bigpicture/sectors.asp?cycle=2004.

were distributed between the Republican and Democratic parties. The most obvious feature of Table 3.5 is the dominance of the business sector. It is far larger than any other single category, providing almost 60 percent of overall contributions, exceeding the combined amount of the other four (nonbusiness) sectors by $714 million. Even more dramatic is the extent of the business sector's superiority in donations compared to organized labor. Union members' donations of $61 million are paltry compared to the $1 billion donated by business-identified individuals. There can be no mistaking the fact that the funding of electoral campaigns in the United States is undertaken primarily on behalf of corporate America. The people who pay for U.S. politics are overwhelmingly rich men whose principal occupational identification is their attachment to American business.

Table 3.5 not only reveals the differences between the two major parties, but also indicates how similar they are with regard to their funding sources. On the one hand, it is obvious that the Republican Party is much more dependent than the Democratic Party on individual contributors who have been coded as representing business firms. While 70 percent of the funds received by Republicans came from this source, 47 percent of the money going to Democrats came from the business sector. In every category except business, the Democrats raise more money than do the Republicans. This is particularly clear in the case of the Lawyers/Lobbyists category, where Democrats received about $150 million compared to the approximately $60 million received by Republicans. As a result, the Democrats were able to raise about the same amount of money as the Republicans, $858 million compared to $871 million.

At the same time, however, the similarities between the parties also are obvious. Both are decisively dependent upon corporate financing. It is true that Republicans receive more business money than do Democrats and receive proportionately more of their financing from this source than do Democrats. Nevertheless, it remains the case that the corporate sector is the single most important source of Democratic Party funding. No other category comes close to the $402 million that the business sector contributes to it. Even within the business sector there is a similarity in the funding base of the two parties. Though not shown in Table 3.5 the subcategory Finance, Insurance and Real Estate is the leading business contributor for both parties, providing Republicans with $197 million and Democrats with $140 million. Though it is true that unionists contribute almost exclusively to the Democrats, it is nevertheless the case that even the Democrats rely much more heavily on business donations than on contributions from people in organized labor.

Perhaps most important of all, the political attitudes of the donor elite do not correspond to those of the population as

Table 3.6. Political position of campaign donors on selected issues (%)

	Conservative position	Neutral	Liberal position
Tax cuts even if it means reducing government services	51	12	37
More spending to reduce poverty and hunger	45	18	38
U.S. needs national health insurance	49	14	37

Source: Peter L. Francia, John C. Green, Paul S. Hernson, Lynda W. Powell, and Clyde Wilcox, *The Financiers of Congressional Elections* (New York: Columbia University Press, 2003), Table 3, 4, p. 61.

a whole. Political contributors are more conservative than is the general population. In contrast to the public's support for programs to achieve greater income equality, "most donors," as Francia et al. put it, "are conservative on economic [and] social-welfare ... " issues.[13] They support cutbacks in social spending, oppose spending to alleviate poverty and hunger, and oppose a national health insurance system (Table 3.6). To be sure, not all wealthy individuals are in political agreement with each other. Nevertheless, there is a central tendency in ideology among this group, and it falls to the political right of the rest of the population.

[13] Francia et al., *The Financiers of Congressional Elections*, p. 60.

Thus, there is a dramatic split between the political attitudes of the electorate and those of the groups that fund the political system. In the present context, it is not an exaggeration to say that those who pay for the political system are opposed to interventions to offset inequality, while large numbers of the electorate favor such schemes. What still needs to be explained are the mechanisms by which these preferences have been realized in policy and, in particular, why the American electorate has been willing to go along with neglect in this policy area.

4

History and Reform Efforts

Concern with the role of private funding in the American political process has a long history, and in recent years serious efforts at reform have been made. But at least to date, public funding of congressional races has not been adopted. In order to understand this country's outlier status in this regard, it is useful to review its experience with political campaign funding.

Lack of data makes it impossible to state definitively who historically paid for electoral campaigns in the United States. Campaign financing, in the words of Frank J. Sorauf, "has always been the *terra incognita* of American politics."[1]

---

[1] Frank J. Sorauf, *Money in American Elections* (Glenview, IL: Scott, Foresman, 1988), p. 17. Thomas Ferguson, a pioneer in the study of the financing of American politics, agrees, noting that only fragmentary data are available concerning the financing of politics "for nearly all periods of American history." Nonetheless, Ferguson belives that this absence "is less devastating to political analysis than it appears" since it is possible to use archival and published material to construct general patterns of financing. See Thomas Ferguson, *Golden Rule: The Investment Theory of Party*

Nonetheless, what is known is that throughout the nineteenth century and into the 1930s and 1940s, the financing of races for office was principally the responsibility of political parties and not, as is the case at present, that of individual candidates. The lack of systematic information makes it difficult to be certain which of the two ways that parties raised funds in those years was more important: voluntary contributions made by wealthy donors or the obligatory payments made by individuals who had been granted jobs or favors by their party.

During the 1890s, the Gilded Age of American politics, the obligatory component of party finance, according to Mark Wahlgen Summers, took the form of assessments on "office-holders in particular and partisans in general." Candidates for office were required to pay what was in effect an entry fee, with the amount due to the party scaled to the compensation level they would receive if they were victorious. As Summers puts it, "the more lucrative or prestigious the office was, the bigger the amount a party levied on the nominee."[2] But it was not only party candidates who were expected to provide funding. Quid pro quos were required from appointees to government jobs as well. Summers reports that "the loyal partisan was expected

---

Competition and the Logic of Money-Driven Political Systems (Chicago and London: University of Chicago Press, 1995), pp. 40–1.

[2] Quotations in this and the following paragraph come from Mark Wahlgren Summers, "'To Make the Wheels Revolve We Must Have Grease': Barrel Politics in the Gilded Age," in Paula Baker (ed.), *Money and Politics* (University Park: Pennsylvania State University Press, 2002), pp. 59–61.

to pay some of his or her salary to campaign funds" and that "no salary was too modest to be overlooked, from municipal scrubwomen to disabled inmates of soldiers' homes and jailhouse wardens."

But this institutionalized system of kickbacks was never the sole or, if anecdotal evidence is to be believed, the most important source of party financing. Businessmen throughout U.S. history have played an important role in political funding. Summers, for example, provides a long list of business owners who made major contributions to the Democratic Party for Grover Cleveland's 1884 presidential campaign, though he is unable to determine how much overall was raised from such sources and compare it to the total raised by Democrats in that year. What he can say is that "the parties usually could count on large contributions" from "a broad array of monied men." This source of funding was particularly important for candidates who were not themselves wealthy. They required, as Summers puts it, "businessmen of some means or . . . rich friends to back them."

Through the 1920s, this pattern showed little change. Parties still tried to raise the money they needed to fund campaigns from candidates and individuals who held appointed office. Writing in 1932, Louise Overacker reports that "assessments upon candidates and voluntary or enforced contributions from office holders form the backbone of the funds handled by many state committees." And though the professionalization of the federal civil service had reduced the vulnerability of government employees to compulsory contributions, she reports that funds still were required from "the army of public employees who owe their position to appointment of the party in power" at the state and local levels. Civil servants, she writes, still were "the prey of local, state and national committees and their contributions – sometimes 'voluntary' and some times otherwise – have been an important source of party funds."[3]

Notwithstanding the importance of this form of semicoerced financing, these funds were insufficient to meet the needs of the major political parties. Parties required large contributions from rich donors as well. Writing about the Republican State Committee in 1920, Overacker reports that "the part which the rank and file took in financing the campaign was insignificant and . . . the party would have been embarrassed . . . without its plutocrats." Contributions of $5,000 or more, a level that in that year represented a very large financial commitment indeed, constituted about half of the contributions received by the two major parties in 1928. Overacker concludes that "the evidence is overwhelming that most of the money with which the major parties wage their state campaigns is contributed by the few rather than the many." She

---

[3] Louise Overacker, *Money in Elections* (New York: Macmillan, 1932), pp. 126, 101–2.

Table 4.1. Total real political spending ($ billions) in presidential election years, 1952–80

Year	Current $ spending	Consumer price index (1982–4 = 100)	Constant $ spending	Four year percent change
1952	.140	26.6	.526	
1956	.155	27.2	.570	+8.4
1960	.175	29.6	.591	+3.7
1964	.200	31.1	.643	+8.8
1968	.300	34.8	.862	+34.1
1972	.425	41.8	1.017	+18.0
1976	.540	56.9	.949	−6.7
1980	1.200	82.3	1.458	+53.7

Source: Spending: Herbert E. Alexander, *Financing Politics: Money, Elections and Political Reform*, 3rd ed., (Washington, DC: CQ Press, 1984), Fig. 1-2, p. 11; Consumer price index: *Statistical Abstract of the United States, 2004–2005* (Washington, DC: Government Printing Office, 2005), Table 697, p. 461.

goes on to say that a "very large part of what goes into these [party] war chests comes from very wealthy individuals who are not themselves seekers after office."[4]

This dependence on wealthy donors intensified with the passage of time, particularly because campaign costs increased rapidly from the 1950s on. The earliest estimates of total campaign spending are those made by Herbert E. Alexander for the years 1952 to 1980. Table 4.1 adjusts Alexander's estimates to take into account the price levels in those years

[4] Ibid., pp. 126, 143, 129.

compared to the present – converting current dollar estimates into constant dollar estimates. As reported in that table, campaign costs in 1964 were 22 percent higher than they had been in 1952; between 1964 and 1968 alone they jumped by more than one-third; and then they increased by another 18 percent between 1968 and 1972. Though this upswing was reversed in 1976, it resumed with an even more dramatic increase of more than 50 percent between 1976 and 1980.

The increased use of radio and television advertising was the most important reason for the need for additional funds. In 1952 only about one-third of American households owned television sets. In contrast, by 1964, virtually all did (92 percent). The result was, according to Frank J. Sorauf, "a revolution in campaign politics."[5] Television exposure became the central focus of campaign activity.

It was in the context of these escalating campaign costs that the era of campaign finance reform began. Direct corporate political contributions had been banned in 1907, and the first federal campaign disclosure law had been adopted in 1910. But no new legislation followed for more than a half-century. As Alexander puts it, "for decades official apathy toward serious reform of political finance was a Washington habit."[6] But

---

[5] Sorauf, *Money in American Elections*, pp. 25–6.

[6] Herbert E. Alexander, *Financing Politics: Money, Elections and Political Reform*, 3rd ed. (Washington, DC: CQ Press, 1984), p. 31.

with campaign costs rising and increasing anxiety on the part
of incumbents that they might become vulnerable to wealthy
challengers, the issue came alive. President John F. Kennedy
responded in 1961 by appointing a bipartisan Commission on
Campaign Costs.[7] In its press release announcing the creation
of the commission, the White House insisted that its goal was
to replace big contributors, not to do away with private funding altogether. To this end, the commission's report sought as
well to reduce campaign costs and to create a mechanism by
which campaign contributions and expenditures were made
public. As Alexander, who himself directed the staff of the commission, suggests, the purpose of its report was "to get things
moving in this area of legislation by detailing a comprehensive
program for reform."[8]

Nothing came of this effort for almost a decade. But in 1971,
Congress passed the Federal Election Campaign Act (FECA),
which President Richard M. Nixon signed in February 1972.
This law tightened revenue-reporting requirements and limited expenditures on media advertising in congressional campaigns to $50,000 or 10 cents per voting-age resident. In the
same year, legislation creating a system of public funding for
presidential elections was also adopted. However, the latter's
implementation was delayed until 1976, by which time its

[7] Sorauf, *Money in American Elections*, p. 35.
[8] Alexander, *Financing Politics*, p. 33.

provisions had been superseded by the landmark legislation of the period, the FECA amendments of 1974.[9]

The latter, though technically only amending the 1971 legislation, in fact initiated a new era of campaign financing. The act strengthened the disclosure provisions of the 1971 act, limited both contributions to and expenditures by political campaigns, established a voluntary system by which candidates for the presidency could run for office using public funds, and created the Federal Election Commission to administer the new system.[10] It was, as Anthony Corrado has put it, "the most comprehensive reform of the campaign finance system ever adopted."[11]

The complete history of this dramatic change in direction resulting in the passage of FECA has not yet been written. But in his pioneering work on this subject, Julian E. Zelizer identifies four separate factors that came together to produce the passage of reform.[12] First, "at the heart of the struggle" was a reform coalition "composed of legislators, experts, philanthropists,

---

[9] Anthony Corrado, "Money and Politics: A History of Federal Campaign Finance Law," in Anthony Corrado, Thomas E. Mann, Daniel R. Ortiz, Trevor Potter, and Frank J. Sorauf (eds.), *Campaign Finance Reform: A Sourcebook* (Washington, DC: Brookings Institution Press, 1997), pp. 50–3.

[10] It also eliminated the media spending limits contained in the 1971 legislation.

[11] Corrado, *"Money and Politics,"* p. 53

[12] The quotations in this paragraph are taken from Julian E. Zelizer, "Seeds of Cynicism: The Struggle Over Campaign Finance, 1956–1974," in Baker, *Money and Politics* pp. 74, 75.

foundations and public interest groups." Though this coalition never built strong grassroots support for the issue, it nevertheless was able to place it on the national agenda. Second, these efforts, he maintains, were joined by political self-interest. Zelizer points out that through the 1960s, the cost of political advertising on television had been increasing at the very time that the financial condition of the major political parties was in decline. Thus, legislators were eager to find ways to contain campaign costs. Third, Zelizer notes the existence of "a new adversarial media." This, he believes, created the perception that opposing reform might be politically dangerous for incumbents. When finally the political interest in reform that these three were responsible for was reinforced by a fourth factor – the Watergate scandal – officeholders quickly passed campaign finance reform because they feared "an angry constituency prepared to remove them from office." Thus, on August 8, 1974, a few hours before President Nixon announced his resignation, the House of Representatives passed a new campaign finance law. President Gerald R. Ford signed it on October 15, 1974, declaring that though he opposed parts of the law, he nevertheless agreed that "the times demand this legislation."[13]

The constitutionality of the law was argued before the Supreme Court in late 1975, and the Court ruled on the act in

---

[13] Quoted in Alexander, *Financing Politics*, p. 38.

its *Buckley v. Valeo* decision on January 30, 1976.[14] The Court's majority agreed that the government had a legitimate interest in eliminating corruption or the appearance of corruption in the political system. It maintained that "to the extent that large contributions are given to secure a political quid pro quo from current and potential office holders, the integrity of our system of representative democracy is undermined." Since, as the Court put it, the problem that Congress addressed with FECA was "not an illusory one. . . . ", it was acceptable for Congress to act to eliminate "the real or imagined coercive influence of large financial contributions on candidates' positions and on their actions if elected to office."

What the Court ruled as unacceptable, however, was limiting speech in the name of "equalizing the relative ability of individuals and groups to influence the outcome of elections." It elaborated: "the concept that government may restrict the speech of some elements of our society in order to enhance the relative voice of others is wholly foreign to the First Amendment. . . . "

Applying this reasoning, the Court ruled that Congress had not overstepped the Constitution in restricting campaign contributions, but that FECA did violate the Constitution

---

[14] Quotations from the Buckley v. Valeo decision are taken from the Electronic Privacy Information Center, http://www.epic.org/free_speech/Buckley_v_Valeo.html.

in imposing restrictions on expenditures. Its argument was that limiting contributions "entails only a marginal restriction upon the contributor's ability to engage in free communication" but that, in contrast, spending limits were "substantial... restraints on the quantity and diversity of political speech." According to the Court, "a restriction on the amount of money a person or group can spend on political communication during a campaign necessarily reduces the quantity of expression by restricting the number of issues discussed, the depth of their exploration and the size of the audience reached." But at the same time, it ruled that limits on contributions are less burdensome because "a contribution serves [only] as a general expression of support for the candidate and his views, but does not communicate the underlying basis for support."

With the FECA Amendments enacted, donors were not permitted to make political donations of more than $25,000 per year or $50,000 per election cycle.[15] Contributions by individuals to federal office seekers were limited to $2,000 per election cycle. Individual contributions to PACs were also limited, to $10,000 per election cycle. In addition, contributions to state party committees were capped at $10,000 per election cycle, with the election cycle limit for individual donations to

---

[15] An election cycle includes both the primary election and the general election.

71

national party committees set at $40,000.[16] Corporations and unions were barred from making direct contributions, but no restrictions at all were imposed on spending by candidates.

The Court also found that FECA's voluntary public financing system for presidential elections was constitutionally acceptable. In this context too the Court affirmed the objective of reducing "the deleterious influence of large contributions on our political process" as well as facilitating "communications by candidates with the electorate and ... free[ing] candidates from the rigors of fundraising." Concerning the expenditures involved, the Court ruled that "Congress has the power to regulate Presidential elections and primaries ... and public financing of presidential elections as a means to reform the electoral process was clearly a choice within the granted power."

It did not take long, however, for candidates and political parties to find ways around the new contribution rules. Despite the fact that the new law required electoral campaigns to be funded with restricted donations ("hard money"), unregulated contributions ("soft money") more and more were used surreptitiously for this purpose. By the mid-1990s it had become clear that the limits on contributions contained in FECA were simply not doing their job. As a 1998 Senate Committee on

---

[16] Joseph E. Cantor and L. Page Whitaker, "Bipartisan Campaign Reform Act of 2002: Summary and Comparison with Previous Law," *Report for Congress, Received through the CRS Web* (Washington, DC: Congressional Research Service, Library of Congress, January 31, 2003), CRS-2.

Governmental Affairs put it, soft money had created a "melt-down" of the campaign finance system created by FECA.[17]

The soft money loophole emerged because the *Buckley* decision required reporting and contribution limits only for "communications that expressly advocate the election or defeat of a clearly identified candidate." In interpreting this phrase, the Court differentiated between "express advocacy," for which contribution limits were imposed, and "issue advocacy," for which they were not. To operationalize that distinction, the Court defined express advocacy to "include explicit words of advocacy of election or defeat of a candidate." This came to be known as the "magic words" requirement. Only if words such as "vote for," "elect," "support," or "reject" were included would an advertisement be subject to FECA rules. Advertisements that did not use those words were unregulated and thus could be purchased with soft money. The problem was that it was easy to create ads that avoided the use of the magic words but nevertheless conveyed a strong message of candidate support or opposition.[18]

Soft money became particularly important for the Democratic Party. As indicated in Table 4.2, in 1991–2 this source

---

[17] Quoted in Supreme Court of the United States, 540 US, 2003, *McConnell, United States Senator et al. v. Federal Election Commission et al.*", http://www.caselaw.lp.findlaw.com/cgi-bin/getcase.pl?court=US&navby=case&vol=000&invol=02-1674#opinion1, p. 19. Hereafter cited as *McConnell v. FEC.*

[18] Ibid., 15, 83–4.

Table 4.2. Soft and hard money contribution to parties, 1991–2 and 2001–2 ($millions)

	Democratic party		Republican party	
	Soft	*Hard*	*Soft*	*Hard*
1991–2	36.3	163.3	49.8	264.9
2001–2	246.1	217.2	250.0	424.1

Source: Harold W. Stanley and Richard G. Niemi, *Vital Statistics on American Politics, 2005–06* (Washington, DC: CQ Press, 2006), Table 10.

of financing was of relatively minor importance for both dominant parties. Ten years later, however, the Democratic Party actually received more unregulated money than regulated contributions. Soft money was less important to the Republican Party. Even so, unregulated contributions to the GOP also grew more than did regulated contributions and became an important source of funding for that party as well. The intent of FECA thereby was thwarted.

Plugging this soft money loophole was Congress's primary intention in passing the 2002 McCain–Feingold bill (formally known as the Bipartisan Campaign Reform Act – BCRA). BCRA banned the solicitation and use of unregulated soft money funds by national parties and candidates for federal office. At the same time, it raised the amount of regulated hard money that individuals could contribute to candidates, parties, and PACs from $50,000 per election cycle to $95,000.

Under BCRA, individuals could now contribute $4,000 to individual candidates per election cycle rather than $2,000, as under FECA; $25,000 instead of $20,000 to individual party committees; and $10,000 instead of $5,000 to state or local party committees.[19]

In creating a new concept, "electioneering communication," and replacing "express advocacy" with it, BCRA redefined the kind of advertising that would be subject to control. As defined by BCRA, electioneering activities that now were to be subject to regulation were broadcast, cable, or satellite advertisements that could be seen by 50,000 people in a district or state and that made any reference to a candidate (not necessarily endorsing or opposing). Unregulated funds could not be used to pay for such advertisements either sixty days before a general election or thirty days before a primary poll. Unions and corporations were barred altogether from using their funds for such communications. In addition, the source of funds for advertisements paid for with "hard money had to be fully disclosed."[20]

As had been the case with FECA, the Supreme Court closely scrutinized BCRA's constitutionality in a case known as *McConnell v. FEC*. In this ruling the Court endorsed BCRA in the same general terms that it had applied to FECA. It appealed

[19] Cantor and Whitaker, "Bipartisan Campaign Reform Act of 2002," CRS-2.
[20] *McConnell v. FEC*, p. 82.

to the need to eliminate corruption and the appearance of corruption in the political system. The Court made it clear that its use of the term corruption was expansive and that its fundamental concern was with the disproportionate power of wealth in politics. It explicitly warned against conceiving of "corruption too narrowly," declaring that "just as troubling to a functioning democracy as classic *quid pro quo* corruption is the danger that officeholders will decide issues not on the merits of the desires of the constituencies but according to the wishes of those who have made large financial contributions valued by the officeholders." It noted that "the evidence connects soft money to manipulations of the legislative calendar, leading to Congress' failure to enact, among other things, generic drug legislation tort reform and tobacco legislation." The majority of the justices believed that political contributions provided donors with access to political decision makers, and "to claim that such actions do not change legislative outcomes surely misunderstands the legislative process."[21]

Specifically, the Court found that the use of the magic words test had not been successful in identifying express advocacy. It wrote: "the unmistakable lesson from the record in this litigation is that Buckley's magic–words requirement is functionally meaningless." As the Court put it, "although the resulting advertisements do not urge the viewer to vote for or against a

[21] Ibid., pp. 43–4, 40.

candidate in so many words, they are no less clearly intended to influence the election." What particularly exercised the Court in this regard was the behavior of unions and corporations. According to the Court, "the factual record demonstrates that the abuse of the present law not only permits corporations and labor unions to fund broadcast advertisements designed to influence federal elections, but permits them to do so while concealing their identities from the public."[22]

But in a subsequent decision, the Supreme Court backed away from this blanket endorsement of BCRA. The Court ruled in the *FEC v. Wisconsin Right to Life Appeal* that the restrictions contained in the law on political advocacy are subject to strict scrutiny. Rather than accepting a broad definition of electioneering communications the Court now argued that if advertisements could "reasonably be interpreted as something other than an appeal to vote for or against a specific candidate, they are not the functional equivalent of express advocacy and therefore fall outside of *McConnell*'s scope." With this reasoning, the Court ruled that three broadcast advertisements paid for by Wisconsin Right to Life that told voters to contact Senators Russell D. Feingold and Herb Kohl and urge them to oppose a senatorial filibuster blocking judicial nominees were genuine issue ads that could not be constitutionally barred.[23]

---

[22] Ibid., pp. 86, 89.

[23] *Federal Election Commission v. Wisconsin Right to Life Inc.*, Appeal from the United States District Court for the District of Columbia, No. 06–969,

In reporting on this case, the *New York Times* quoted experts as saying that the decision "undercut the soft money section" of BCRA and permitted "a largely unlimited flow of money from corporate treasuries" to pay for advertisements in the weeks before primary and general elections.[24] But the fact is that, as had been the case with FECA, techniques had already been developed to evade the intent of BCRA. Unregulated political expenditures had not disappeared because of that law, though they took a different form and were reduced in scale.

Probably the most important evasive method involved donations to groups called 527s[25] – political organizations whose purpose was to influence elections at the federal or national level. As such, they would be subject to BCRA contribution limits. But donors who wanted to circumvent BCRA could make their contributions to "nonfederal accounts" held by these organizations. Nonfederal activities such as support for candidates at the state or local level are not regulated by BCRA, and so, the argument went, there were no limitations on contributions to them. The problem is that these unregulated

June 25, 2007, http://caselaw.lp.findlaw.com/scripts/printer_friendly.pl?page=000/06-969.html.

[24] Linda Greenhouse and David D. Kirkpatrick, "Justices Loosen Ad Restrictions in Campaign Law," *The New York Times*, June 26, 2007, http://www.nytimes.com.

[25] The name 527s refers to the section of the Internal Revenue Service tax code that governs these organizations.

funds were in fact used in federal elections. As a result, a new form of soft money electioneering emerged. The 527s have used unregulated money in nonfederal accounts to influence elections at the national level, something that BCRA requires be done only with hard money.[26]

Despite this circumvention, BCRA did reduce the role of unregulated funds in the election process in the 2004 election cycle and increase the role of regulated funds. What it did not do was undermine the power of wealth in the political process. The donor elite continued to dominate.

Table 4.3 uses data provided by the Center for Responsive Politics to compare the role of unregulated money in the 2000 and 2004 elections. As we have seen, BCRA banned unregulated money from being provided to candidates. No such funds, therefore, are recorded in the table for 2004. Nevertheless unregulated money still was present in the form of independent spending by interest groups, candidate self-financing, and of course the spending by 527s. The table reveals that BCRA did have an effect on soft money. Notwithstanding the emergence of 527s, unregulated contributions fell from over $900 million in 2000, representing almost one-third (29.7 percent) of all expenditures, to $530 million in 2004, only 13.7 percent of total outlays in that year. In contrast, regulated

---

[26] Jay R. Mandle, "What is a 527?" *Money on My Mind*, March 2004, http://www.democracymatters.org.

Table 4.3. Funding levels by source for election in 2000 and 2004
($ millions)

	2000		2004	
	Amount	Percent of total	Amount	Percent of total
Total expenditures	3,042	100.0	3,862	100.0
Unregulated				
Soft money	499	16.4	–	–
Independent spending by interest groups	200	6.6	–	–
Candidate self-financing	205	6.7	144	3.7
527 spending	–	–	386	10.0
Total unregulated	**903**	**29.7**	**530**	**13.7**
Regulated				
Individual contributions to candidates and parties	1,460	48.0	2,500	64.7
PAC contributions to candidates and parties	288	9.5	384	10.0
Total regulated	**1,748**	**57.5**	**2,884**	**74.7**
Other[a]	**391**	**12.8**	**448**	**11.7**

[a] Public funds to presidential candidates and parties, other candidates' revenues, convention host committee spending.

Source: Center for Responsive Politics, http://www.opensecrets.org/pressreleases/2004/04spending.asp.

contributions, donations by individuals or PACs, increased from $1.748 billion in 2000 to $2.884 billion in 2004. About three-quarters of all expenditures in 2004 were subject to limits, while in 2000 regulated expenditures represented 57.4 percent. In this regard, BCRA accomplished its objective. The role of soft money was reduced.

But strengthening control over campaign donations should not be confused with democratizing the funding of the political process. The argument that BCRA might result in such a change was based on the assumption that limiting contributions from traditional donors by imposing hard money limits would reduce their importance. If this were the case, and if at the same time the costs of political campaigns continued to rise, candidates would feel pressure to augment their funding sources and would then seek funds from a wider donor pool. Indeed, Lawrence Noble and Steven Weiss report that precisely such a mechanism was operative after the passage of BCRA. They write, "the new law banned unlimited 'soft' money contributions to the political parties, forcing party leaders to ramp up their efforts to collect donations in amounts of $200 or less. They appear to have done so."[27]

In fact, however, it is not possible to be definitive concerning the extent to which the small donor base expanded in

[27] Lawrence Noble and Steven Weiss, "Op-Ed: Plenty of Individual Contributions," as published in the *Miami Herald*, November 25, 2004, http://www.opensecrets.org/prereleases/2004/Elections CostOpEd.asp

reaction to BCRA. Available evidence, however, suggests that any movement in this direction was inadequate to dethrone the role of big donors. The growth in the importance of small contributors was nowhere near sufficient to materially undermine the dominance of large contributors.

Under the law, political contributions of less than $200 – considered here to be small donations – do not have to be itemized by their recipients. As a result, no direct count of such donors is possible. At best, therefore, an assessment of the role of small donors involves comparing the number of donors who contributed more than $200 (for which we do possess firm data) with estimates of those who contributed less than that amount.

Such estimates have been prepared by the Institute for Politics, Democracy and the Internet (IPDI) and are reported in Tables 4.4 and 4.5. The data show that an important increase in the role of small donors did occur in the 2004 election. Small donor contributions increased from about $38 million in 2000 to over $200 million in 2004. If the IPDI estimates are accurate – an assumption that seems to correspond to anecdotal evidence but that cannot be definitively proven – this increase mostly reflected a fourfold growth in the number of such donors and, to a much lesser extent, was the consequence of an increase in the mean contribution of small donors. As a result, the share that small donors contributed to the total income received by politicians and parties increased from

Table 4.4. Political contributors by level of contribution, 2000

	Amount (millions of $)	Percent of total individual contributions to candidates and parties	Number of donors	Donors as percent of adult population
Total	1,275	100.0	1,403,616	0.67
$10,000+	446	35.0	14,906	0.01
$200–9,999	791	62.0	763,710	0.36
Less than $200[a]	38	3.0	625,000	0.30

[a] Estimate: For Source: see below.

Source: Donations of $10,000+ and $200–9,999: calculated from data at http://www.opensecrets.org/bigpicture/DonorDemographics.asp?Cycle=2000 and http://www.opensecrets.org/bigpicture/DonorDemographics.asp?Cycle=2004. Estimate for Less than $200: Institute for Politics, Democracy and the Internet, "Small Donors and Online Giving," p. 5; total is summation of $10,000+, $200–9,999, and Less than $200.

3.0 percent to 9.7 percent. The flip side of this increase was the declines in the importance of the biggest donors ($10,000+) from 35.0 percent to 30.4 percent and that of the middle category ($200–$9,999) from 62.0 percent to 59.9 percent. The IPDI was not far wrong in reporting that "the dramatic growth story for 2004 came in the number of small donors."[28]

However, it remains the case that the financing of electoral races in the United States continues to be overwhelmingly

[28] Institute for Politics, Democracy and the Internet, *Small Donors and Online Giving: A Study of Donors to the 2004 Presidential Campaigns* (Washington DC: George Washington University Press, March 2006), p. 5.

Table 4.5. Number and amount of individual contributions to parties, candidates, and PACs, 2004

	Amount (millions of $)	Percent of total individual contributions to candidates and parties	Number of donors	Donors as percent of adult population
Total	2,120	100.0	3,941,183	1.78
$10,000+	644	30.4	25,824	0.01
$200–9,999	1,270	59.9	1,115,359	0.50
Less than $200[a]	206	9.7	2,800,000	1.27

[a] Estimate: for source see below.

Source: See Table 4.4.

dependent on large contributions from a very small segment of the adult population. Even after the big influx of small donors, Table 4.5 reveals that less than 2 percent of adults (1.78 percent) were responsible for all the money that parties and candidates raised. But even more, big donors continue to dominate the flow of funds to politicians. As indicated in the table, contributors of $200 or more in the 2004 election cycle, constituting less than 1 percent of the adult population (0.51 percent), contributed 90.3 percent of the funds received.

Thus, while there has been a change in the relative importance of regulated compared to unregulated political donations, and while the importance of small donors has increased, what has not changed is that a very narrow segment of the population continues to provide the funding for electoral campaigns. Particularly telling in this regard is the continuing importance of big donors. Facilitated by the provisions in BCRA that increased the amount of money that individuals could contribute to candidates and parties, the donations of those providing $10,000 or more grew by 44 percent between 2000 and 2004. What this means is that office seekers are still primarily dependent on large donors and must ensure that their big contributors remain supportive. Even in 2004, after the increased role of small donors, the number of under-$200 contributors would have had to have increased by another 300 percent – to almost 8 million from less than 3 million – to replace the money provided by the roughly 26,000 people who made large donations.

In short, the financing of the American political process remains in the hands of a small elite. If the goal of the reform effort had been to break that control, it clearly failed. The continued disproportionate impact of private wealth means that corruption, as broadly defined by the Supreme Court, remains endemic. Politics still is largely paid for and therefore is excessively influenced by the rich.

5

Distrust of Government

All societies engage in politics, and all political systems require resources. An adequate supply of people and equipment must be mobilized so that collective decisionmaking – the substance of the political process – can be undertaken. Politics is costly. There is no free lunch.

In a political system like ours, in which officeholders are elected, each candidate for office needs financing in order to mount a campaign. At the most elementary level, campaign flyers or posters providing information about a candidate require paper that has to be bought and printing services that have to be paid for. The finished printed materials must be distributed, involving transportation costs. Today, television campaign commercials must be produced and air time purchased – both fabulously expensive propositions. Even a minimal television advertising campaign costs thousands of dollars. Without the money to do these and myriad other things, would-be officeholders simply have no chance of political success. Unable to raise adequate funds, a candidate will not be able to communicate effectively with the electorate, dooming his or her chances of victory. Very rarely do citizens vote for candidates about whom they have little or no information and with whom they are unfamiliar.

In the absence of public funds, there is only one recourse for electoral candidates. Unless they are enormously wealthy and can pay for their races themselves, all office seekers must solicit donations from individuals and PACs. As we have seen, an elaborate cat-and-mouse game has been played in recent years in order to stretch, if not evade, the laws governing campaign financing. But even as the legal context has changed – first with FECA and then with BCRA – one thing has remained constant: political campaigns overwhelmingly are paid for by a tiny wealthy minority of the American people.

If it is obvious why candidates must seek funding, it is no less clear why donors provide such funds. They do so because they seek either ideological or personal gain. Thus, donors may provide money to candidates whom they know to be in policy alignment with themselves and/or to gain influence with a potential legislator. They may seek such influence either to advance their general viewpoint or to obtain preferential treatment in legislation that may be adopted. No one that I know of claims that political donations are made without some form of self-interest involved. Disinterested donors do not provide funds. The hope for political or material advance lies behind the contribution of funds to politicians. Seen in this light, political parties are, as Thomas Ferguson puts it, "blocs of major investors who coalesce to advance candidates representing their interests."[1]

In recent years, political scientists in the United States have produced a voluminous literature attempting to answer the question of what donors obtain in exchange for their contributions. There is very little doubt, as documented in Chapter 3, that political campaigns are funded principally by a relatively small number of wealthy, conservative men. But what does remain in dispute is the extent of the power that these contributions provide to political donors.

A Task Force on American Democracy in an Age of Rising Inequality organized by the American Political Science Association took up this subject and responded in two ways. In the first place, it rejected the view that the U.S. political system is subject to rampant and overt corruption. The authors of the report wrote that "politicians are not usually bribed by political contributors or moneyed interests. Research does not support the idea that specific votes in Congress are directly determined by campaign contributions." However, at the same time that the authors rejected the claim that the political system is a giant bazaar, they indicted that it is unequal. Despite the fact, as they write, that "Americans fervently believe that everyone

---

[1] Thomas Ferguson, *Golden Rule: The Investment Theory of Party Competition and the Logic of Money-Driven Political Systems* (Chicago and London: The University of Chicago Press, 1995), p. 27.

should have an equal say in our democratic politics," the reality is that "as wealth and income have become more concentrated and the flow of money into elections has grown, campaign contributions give the affluent a means to express their voice that is unavailable to most citizens." The report indicates that "what wealthy citizens and moneyed interests do gain from their big contributions" are two valuable prizes: "influence over who runs for office and a hearing from politicians and government officials once they are in positions of authority." As the report puts it, "access for the few can thereby crowd out attention to the many."[2]

Obviously, this is a damning report. It could not be more clear in its assertion that the U.S. political system does not accord each individual an equal opportunity to influence political outcomes. But even as it makes this case, the Task Force is excessively complacent about corruption. The authors frame the issue as whether politicians "usually" are bribed and whether votes are "directly determined" by campaign contributions. Portraying the issue in such stark terms makes it all but inevitable that the members of Congress will be exonerated from the charge of venality. "Usually" and "directly" are very demanding criteria to be met before the charge of corruption can be made to stick. The reality is that there would still be a

---

[2] Task Force on American Democracy in an Age of Rising Inequality (American Political Science Association, http://www.apsanet.org, 2004), pp. 12, 4, 7.

serious problem for democracy if politicians were only sometimes bribed and if legislation were indirectly determined by donations.

Recent cases of congressional corruption not only suggest that this is the case but illustrate that the temptation to corrupt behavior is powerful in our system of private electoral financing. On the assumption that politicians are no more immune to enticements than the rest of the population, the incentive to trade favors for donations in the current system represents a systemic weakness to which the Task Force pays insufficient attention.[3]

The temptations available to members of Congress and the ways political actors circumvent the laws against bribery to make it appear that congressional actions do not represent paybacks are illustrated in the case of Brent T. Wilkes, an associate of Randy Cunningham, the former California member of the House of Representatives who resigned from office after being convicted of accepting bribes and underreporting his income.

As described in a *New York Times* article, Wilkes prepared envelopes for a half dozen members of Congress, each of which contained $10,000 in checks. He was careful not to present the envelopes to the congressmen at the time and in the same room

---

[3] See my "'Earmarks' and National Security," *Money on My Mind*, October 2006, http://www.democracymatters.org.

in which he was lobbying on behalf of his clients. Instead, he handed over the envelopes in the hallway outside the room. In this way, he believed, he avoided illegality. Since, as the article puts it, a committee such as the House Appropriations Subcommittee "is one of great power and little scrutiny" and in which, as Wilkes told the *Times*, "every member appeared to have a personal allowance of millions of dollars to disburse without public disclosure," it was not difficult for the recipients of these donations to deliver contracts and other benefits. Often the form these quid pro quos took was one of the 12,000 earmarks per year that are attached to spending bills. Earmarks are appropriations inserted in spending bills, in the past often anonymously, for specific projects supported by a member of Congress. Wilkes himself, in denying that he had broken the law, agreed that he had participated in a system of "transactional lobbying," a "'cutthroat' system in which campaign contributions were a prerequisite for federal contracts."[4]

Whether or not transactional lobbying is illegal is beside the point. Doing the country's business in this way not only, as *The Times* puts it, "pervert[s] public policy, encourage[s] cronyism and waste[s] federal money," it is also deeply antidemocratic. Policies are adopted in response to financial support rather

---

[4] David Johnston and David D. Kirkpatrick, "Deal Maker Details the Art of Greasing the Palm," *The New York Times*, August 6, 2006. http://www.nytimes.com.

than constituent preferences. It might well be true that the Cunningham scandal is, as the Task Force suggests, atypical. But the problem here is that no one really knows the extent to which this kind of quid pro quo occurs. Furthermore, knowledge of its pervasiveness is impossible to obtain. Thus, what we are left with is a system in which, to a degree unknown, transactional lobbying can skirt illegality and, to the extent that it does so successfully, represents a deeply antidemocratic method of legislating.

All of this is in addition to the disproportionate power that the Task Force does acknowledge accrues to political donors. It reports two ways in which this occurs. As the report puts it, first "big contributors have the power to discourage or perhaps suffocate unfriendly candidates by denying them early or consistent funding." Second, providing funds earns "the privilege of regularly meeting with policymakers" after the election. Contributors thereby gain a level of access to legislators unavailable to members of the general public. Donors are provided with a privileged opportunity to influence the thinking and actions of officeholders. What these two mechanisms do is accord the donor elite great influence over the political agenda.

With regard to the second of these mechanisms, the process is obvious. Even when it is not illegal, as the Task Force points out, "money buys the opportunity to present self-serving information or raise some problems for attention rather than others."[5] In this regard, Larry M. Bartels has recently provided convincing evidence of the extent to which wealth is associated with power. Bartels relates roll call votes to the opinions of survey respondents in which the opinions of the latter are differentiated by income level. Bartels finds that senators are "vastly more responsive to the views of affluent constituents than to constituents of modest means." He goes on, "Senators seem to have been quite responsive to the ideological views of their middle- and high-income constituents – though, strikingly, *not* to the views of their low-income constituents." Indeed, he concludes, " ... the data are quite consistent in suggesting that the opinion of constituents in the bottom third of the income distribution had *no* discernible impact on the voting behavior of their Senators." Not surprisingly, Bartels also finds that senators were more responsive to their high-income than to their middle income constituents. The consistency with which Bartels finds senators responsive to the wealthy leads him to conclude that "the data are consistent with the hypothesis that senators represented their campaign contributors to the exclusion of other constituents."[6]

Journalistic evidence of such a pattern is extensive. Micah L. Sifry and Nancy Watzman, for example, have compiled a book-length set of examples of how the political process has

---

[5] Task Force on American Democracy, in an Age of Rising Inequality, p. 12.

[6] Larry M. Bartels, "Economic Inequality and Political Representation" (revised August 2005), p. 29, http://www.princeton.edu/~bartels/papers.htm.

shaped policies in the direction sought by campaign contributors. Their examples are telling: Medicare is barred from negotiating lower drug prices from pharmaceutical houses; banking interests benefit from the removal of firewalls preventing potential conflicts of interests; accounting rules and procedures are relaxed; in the face of mounting evidence of global warming, only minimal restraints on greenhouse gas emissions are legislated; energy policy is rigged in favor of the petroleum interests even at the expense of national security concerns; occupational safety problems are sidestepped; tax policy is tilted to disproportionately benefit the rich; and bankruptcy law is changed to deny families the same opportunities to escape debt that corporations are permitted. Sifry and Watzman do not exaggerate when they write that "the air we breathe, the food we eat, the health care we receive (or don't receive), all of these are affected, and for the worse, by the influence of money in politics."[7]

But the Task Force does not elaborate sufficiently on the implication of the first of these mechanisms – the power to determine who does and who does not run for office. The issue here is that all candidates for office know that political contributions are voluntary. They are – they must be – constantly aware that a misstep puts them at risk of losing access to such

[7] Micah L. Sifry and Nancy Watzman, *Is That a Politician in Your Pocket? Washington on $2 Million a Day* (Hoboken, NJ: Wiley, 2004), p. 1.

donations. If such losses are sufficiently extensive, a candidate's viability is destroyed.

What this means is that the donor gains leverage over what the candidate says and stands for. To be sure, an individual donor's leverage is less powerful when an office seeker's funding base is extensive than it is when only a few donors are available. Nevertheless, the power of contributors to withhold funds remains a constant constraining influence on politicians' freedom. The flip side of this situation concerns would-be candidates whose views cannot induce adequate funding. In this case, society suffers when the outcast office seeker's views have merit but are unacceptable to the donor class. If such office seekers cannot raise the money for a campaign, those ideas never become part of the electoral debate.

The point here is that the political agenda is defined as much by what is not articulated as by what is discussed. Because this is so, donors, by virtue of their role in determining who can and cannot run effective political campaigns, possess disproportionate power over the content of political dialogue. It does a politician no good to have great ideas if those ideas are unacceptable to campaign contributors. Promoting such initiatives in the face of opposition from funders risks their alienation, which could prove to be politically fatal to an office seeker. What is worse, because policy innovations are subjected to the test of acceptability to moneyed interests, voters are denied the opportunity to hear the contestants debate the full range of policy possibilities. In short, the private funding of politics constrains the extent and breadth of the political discourse.

With all of this said, it is also obvious that politicians, to be successful, must not ignore the attitudes and preferences of their constituents. Even incumbents can lose at the polls, though this happens infrequently.[8] No funder, however deep his or her pockets, can induce a politician to adopt a position that will result in overwhelming constituency hostility and certain electoral defeat. But voters are able to choose only among the candidates presented to them and must adjudicate among the ideas that those politicians espouse. Voters' sovereignty, therefore, is only a constrained power. Their choices are bounded by the limits imposed by political funders.

Donors have greatest influence on issues about which the public is ignorant. Under those circumstances, or when public sentiment is ill-defined and /or quiescent, the benefits of aligning with the interests of donors come with little risk of a political blowback. There is little likelihood of a negative political reaction if, with regard to the issue at stake, the public is

[8] In 2004, House of Representatives members seeking reelection won in 98.3 percent of the races they entered; the percentage of incumbent victories for senators was 96.2 percent. Harold W. Stanley and Richard G. Niemi, *Vital Statistics on American Politics 2005–2006* (Washington, DC: CQ Press, 2006), Table 1–18.

not actively involved. This is precisely the context that makes the system of congressional earmarks so effective. Projects and expenditures are adopted with no discussion or debate, though in many cases the stakes involved are high. Earmarks represent a secret domain of political choice in which donor power is unchecked.

In this framework, it is possible to explain the inadequacy of the response in the United States to the growth in inequality associated with technological change and globalization. As we have seen, survey data suggest that the absence in this country of robust programs to assist workers displaced by new technology or imports does not reflect the preferences of the population. On the contrary, the political system has not delivered the supportive policies that polling data indicate the population supports and economic change requires. That failure is attributable, it seems clear, to the unobserved power of donors in setting the political agenda and their more overt exercise of influence by lobbying in opposition to ameliorative public spending. The conservative bias built into the U.S. political system by its private funding lies at the root of this country's failure to come to terms with the necessity of ensuring that the victims of technological progress and the spread of economic development are not ignored.

More generally, the conservatism of the donor elite means that the increasingly unequal distribution of income in the

United States is a taboo subject. It does not receive extensive debate because the voices that would raise the issue are largely absent from the political arena because they lack adequate donor support. Furthermore, incumbents and office seekers with a supportive base of contributors are loath to alienate their donors by raising the issue.

Yet, the fact remains that the donor elite is not omnipotent. If a groundswell of popular sentiment for a stronger ameliorative response to the growth in income inequality emerged, it would at least challenge the studied indifference to the subject that prevails among politicians. The puzzle is why the support for income floors and job retraining demonstrated in attitude surveys has not manifested itself politically. It is one thing to say that the funding of our political system biases it against such policies. But it is another thing to point out that there has been very little public activism in support of programs to counter the growth of income inequality.

The political scientist Marc J. Hetherington has emphasized an important point that provides insight into this absence. The American people do not trust the federal government. As Hetherington writes, "even if people support progressive policy goals, they do not support the policies themselves because they do not believe that the government is capable of bringing about desired outcomes." Hetherington believes that the absence of trust has all but killed off the possibility of redistributive programs. He writes, "most Americans simply do not think government is capable of doing the job well enough or fairly enough to help the less well off at the same time [that] it protects the interests of the better off."[9]

To make his case Hetherington uses a "Trust in Government Index" tabulated by the American National Election Studies. Column 1 in Table 5.1 provides an update of that time series. What it reveals is that the present level of the index is much lower than it was forty years ago. This decline occurred primarily between 1966 and 1970, when the Trust in Government Index fell from 61 percent to 39 percent, and then again between 1972 and 1980, when it declined from 38 percent to 27 percent. Thereafter, an irregular but persistent upward trend has occurred. Even so, the 37 percent who reported in 2004 that they trusted the government was far below the levels of the early and middle 1960s.

A key question, not answered in Heatherington's discussion, is what accounts for the long-term downward trend observed in this index. Hetherington provides an anecdotal review of what was occurring politically during these years, in an attempt to match these events with variations in the trend line, but he offers no systematic discussion of why the index has remained far below its initial level.

---

[9] Marc J. Hetherington, *Why Trust Matters: Declining Political Trust and the Demise of American Liberalism* (Princeton, NJ, and Oxford: Princeton University Press, 2005), p. 5.

Distrust of Government

Table 5.1. Trust in government index and percentage of
respondents believing that government is run for the
benefit of a few big interests, 1964–2004

Year	Trust in government index	Government is run for benefit of a few big interests (%)
1964	52	29
1966	61	33
1968	45	40
1970	39	50
1972	38	53
1974	29	66
1976	30	66
1978	29	67
1980	27	70
1982	31	61
1984	38	55
1986	47	Na
1988	34	64
1990	29	71
1992	29	75
1994	26	76
1996	32	69
1998	34	64
2000	36	61
2002	43	48
2004	37	56

Source: The American National Election Studies Guide to Public Opinion
and Electoral Behavior, Tables 5A.5 and 5A.2, http://www.umich.edu/
~nesguide/toptable/tab5a_5.htm.

A possible explanation for the long-term trend, however, is suggested by the data in the far-right column of the table. What is reported there is the percentage of the population that believes, as the survey question puts it, that "the government is pretty much run by a few big interests looking out for themselves." This measure is one of the components of the Trust in Government Index that Heatherington uses. Therefore, it is to be expected that the two measures will tend to move together. Indeed, there is an almost perfect correlation between them.[10] Nevertheless, there is much to be learned by looking separately at the question of whom the public believes the government primarily serves.

The picture that emerges is devastating. Between 1974 and 2004, on average, about two-thirds (64.6 percent) of the American people came to believe that the government is run for the benefit of a few special interests. Furthermore, over time, that belief has risen dramatically. In 1964 less than one-third of respondents believed that that was the case. By 1994 that share had increased to more than three-fourths. Even immediately after the events of September 11, 2001, when there was a drop in the percentage of skeptics concerning the intentions of government, it remained the case that almost one-half of the respondents still believed that the government serves the

---

[10] The correlation coefficient between the two times series in Table 5.1 is 0.94734.

needs of the few, a share that increased to 56 percent in 2004. What these data suggest is that people do not trust the government because they believe that the government benefits a privileged elite.

Support for this view is also provided by an assessment of a different data set by John R. Hibbing and Elizabeth Theiss-Morse. Based on a 1998 survey, they report that more than three-quarters (77 percent) of the sample agree that "special interests" had too much control over what government does. More generally, two-thirds (67 percent) believe that interest groups possess too much power. Three-fifths (60 percent) of the American people either agree or strongly agree that "the American government used to get the job done but not anymore." Finally, just under two-thirds (64 percent) disagree or strongly disagree with the proposition that the current political system does a good job representing the interests of all Americans.[11]

In commenting on these data, Hibbing and Theiss-Morse write that respondents believe that "current political arrangements allow elected officials to play people for suckers." According to the authors, survey participants overwhelmingly believe that politicians receive "enormous benefits from 'special interests' in exchange for granting every wish of these

[11] John R. Hibbing and Elizabeth Theiss-Morse, *Stealth Democracy: Americans' Belief about How Government Should Work* (New York: Cambridge University Press, 2005), Tables 4.2, 4.4, 4.5.

special interests, all the while ignoring the legitimate concerns of the hard-working American people."[12]

Hibbing and Thiess-Morse believe that what bothers the public is not so much that elites are making decisions, but rather that the elites "are willing and able to use their positions to gain personally from the decisions they make." From the perspective of the people polled, they write, "the unholy union of elected officials and special interests is easily the most despised aspect of the American political system." They conclude, "the people, feeling used, absolutely detest this style of decision making and are willing to do virtually anything to avoid it."[13] What, in short, disturbs the public most is exactly the kind of transactional lobbying that was revealed in the Randy Cunningham case.

Hibbing and Theiss-Morse cite representative comments made by a focus group. One person says, "Interest groups control government. The groups with the most amount of money, the most political clout, they say when," and another person responds "I agree with that. I think interest groups...have too much control of what our elected officials say in our government. If you have enough money, and you can give them enough money for their campaigns, then they're going to get

---

[12] John R. Hibbing and Elizabeth Theiss-Morse, "What Would Improve Americans' Attitudes Toward Their Government?" Paper prepared for presentation at the Conference on Trust in Government, Princeton University, November 30–December 1, 2001, p. 8.

[13] Ibid., p. 9.

you to sway your vote . . . I don't understand why some interest groups are allowed to give millions and millions of dollars and other groups can't afford to do that so they are, they can't represent the people they're trying to represent." Summarizing this exchange, Hibbing and Theiss-Morse affirm that "many, many people see special interests at the core of the political system's problems."[14]

The evidence thus suggests that the public finds itself in an immobilizing contradiction. It would like to see the government adopt policies to achieve greater equality in the distribution of income. But at the same time, it believes that it is unlikely to do so because the government is in the pay of a wealthy donor elite. Confronted with the conflict between its goals and its distrust of government as the mechanism to achieve its goals, the electorate has retreated. Not only has it failed aggressively to pursue its egalitarian aspirations, it has largely withdrawn from any kind of political participation at all. The voter turnout rate in the nonpresidential years of 1962 and 1966 averaged 48.2 percent; that statistic for 1998 and 2002 stood at 38.8 percent.[15]

The tension between support for greater equality and dire skepticism that the government can or will act to achieve that goal is played out most dramatically within the Democratic

[14] Hibbing and Theiss-Morse, *Stealth Democracy*, p. 98.
[15] Stanley and Niemi, *Vital Statistics on American Politics*, Table 1-1.

Party. Historically, that party is the inheritor of the legacies of the New Deal and the Great Society. Democrats were primarily responsible for the adoption of the Social Security system in the 1930s and Medicare and Medicaid in the 1960s. Given this history, egalitarians tend to place their hopes with that party. If programs such as wage insurance, portable pension plans, enhanced job retraining, and universal health insurance are to be adopted, the Democratic Party is much more likely to be responsible for their implementation than is the Republican Party.

But its historical ties to the New Deal also mean that the Democratic Party is seen as the party of government. Its historical achievements are embedded in government programs, the very kind viewed with most skepticism today. For this reason, advocates of greater economic equality have a weak hand within the party. To succeed, they will have to devise a strategy that convinces large numbers of Americans that, contrary to what they believe at present, the government can be trusted to address and improve their interests.

The crux of the matter is that if government really is the enemy, then it is literally impossible to do anything about redistribution. This is because only the government can be a counterweight to the market-determined pattern of income distribution. The fact remains, however, that so long as the American people believe that government is a plaything of wealthy political insiders and special interests, it is very hard to envision a political mobilization in support of greater economic equality. Trust in government however could be rehabilitated if the public became convinced that not all politicians were on the take. If that were done, Americans might be similarly convinced that government could act on their behalf and that politicians really might respond to their political preferences. Only then could the country be spared the yawning cleavages in living standards that are currently being created by technological change and globalization in the context of political cynicism. To mount an effective response to growing inequality, Americans must come to believe they truly own the government and that the government will do what they want it to do.

6

The Need for Public Financing

I n the United States, the power of wealth has illegitimately intruded into politics. While democracy should mean that policies are formulated in response to a consensus among citizens of equal political standing, our political system is one of inequality of influence and therefore biased political outcomes. The terms of the social contract required to ensure that justice prevails – namely, that the wealth created in the economy not be accorded disproportionate influence in the world of politics – are not in place. The relationship between the political and economic spheres needs to be reconfigured in order to provide deepened content to American democracy. Such a strengthening requires that the political domain must be equipped to resist the intrusion of private wealth. The problem of how to protect egalitarian politics from the power of wealth is a vexing one. But if political equality is to become a reality, this problem must be solved.

Markets create income inequality. Differences in the availability of and demand for skills mean that some degree of wage inequality will always exist. Since, in addition, the ownership of income-earning property typically is highly concentrated, capital markets are also sources of inequality. There is no escaping the reality that economic inequality is a fact of life in market-dominated economies.

The result is an unavoidable tension between democracy's required egalitarianism and the antiegalitarian pressures that emanate from the economy. The reason for this tension is that the rules governing the economy are written in the political arena. Those rules determine the context in which producers and consumers function. They thus materially influence the likelihood of the business sector's succeeding in achieving its principal objective – earning profits. As a result, managers and entrepreneurs are intensely interested in what goes on politically. It can confidently be predicted that whenever possible and to the extent to which it is feasible, business interests will attempt to shape the content of what emerges from the political process to be consistent with their own economic well-being.

There can be no objection to businesspeople participating in politics in the same way as everyone else. But it is likely that such individuals – with important financial interests at stake – will seek to do more. They will try to find ways to use their wealth to ensure that the weight of their influence on policy outcomes exceeds that of an average politically interested or

The Need for Public Financing

involved citizen.[1] Business executives and managers not only have an incentive to actively try to shape legislation, but typically they possess the financial resources with which to do so.

The use of private wealth in this way, however, subverts political equality. For a politics of equality to be built and maintained, the use of wealth to gain disproportionate influence has to be contained. The political rights of the wealthy have to be respected, but at the same time they have to be denied a privileged political status.

This is the conundrum that the philosopher John Rawls faces when he discusses the threat to political equality that occurs when "those who have greater private means are permitted to use their advantages to control the course of public debate." The "compensating steps" that he recommends to combat that threat include government policies to ensure that property ownership is not excessively concentrated and the use of government money to routinely encourage political debate. In addition, Rawls advocates the public financing of political parties so that they can remain "autonomous with respect to private demands, that is, demands not expressed in the public forum and argued for openly by reference to a conception of the public good." Failure to provide such

---

[1] Gene M. Grossman and Elhanan Helpman, *Special Interest Politics* (Cambridge MA, and London: MIT Press, 2001), p. 344.

resources to political parties will mean that the "pleadings" of donors "are bound to receive excessive attention."[2]

A voluntary system of public funding of electoral campaigns, in the spirit suggested by Rawls, would go far to accomplish this objective. Using tax money to pay the campaign expenses of candidates for office who choose to eschew private donations would diminish the power that wealth presently exercises in determining who runs for public office. With public funding of election campaigns, the lopsided influence of the donor elite in politics would be reduced. As that influence recedes, the political role of the majority of the population – marginalized as it is at present because it is not wealthy – will increase. Because the power of wealth will be substantially walled off from politics, a system that more closely approximates one characterized by political equality would for the first time be realized.

A reform that provides candidates with the option of paying for their campaigns with public funds would involve restructuring the political process. No longer would politics be exclusively a market phenomenon in which donors become consumers paying for the opportunity to influence policy. With public funding of political races, politics would come more to resemble a public good paid for with tax money.

---

[2] John Rawls, *A Theory of Justice* Cambridge, MA: Harvard University Press, (1971), pp. 225, 226.

The Need for Public Financing

Public goods are services that are needed by members of society but that cannot be profitably supplied in adequate amounts by private firms. Typical textbook examples are national defense, the country's system of roads and highways, and local police and fire protection. One reason that public goods are paid for with taxes is that financing them privately would result in their being made disproportionately available to the groups that provide the funding. If that were the case, the resulting distribution of those services would be both inefficient and unfair. Elementary justice suggests that policing, for example, should not be provided primarily to wealthy people who are likely to live in relatively crime-free environments. Rather, it should be supplied most to neighborhoods where crime is extensive, though the people who live in such areas might not be able to pay for the service.

Much the same argument can be made about our political system. With the political process paid for privately, the supply of political services is inevitably most responsive to the interests of large donors. Because of this bias, the distribution of political services is inequitable. In deliberating legislative policies and expenditure levels, policy debates do not focus sufficiently on alternative conceptions of the social good and how best to achieve it. Those debates are polluted by the intrusion of the special interest concerns of those who pay for the process. The problem is that with the private funding of campaigns, such an intrusion is inescapable. The professional viability of political figures requires them to be especially sensitive to the needs of the donor elite. Their careers depend on their satisfying their patrons.

Though not widely recognized, there is already in place in the United States an alternative to a privately funded political system. Voluntary full public funding of election campaigns ("clean elections") has been adopted in recent years in Maine (1996), in Arizona (1998), and most recently in Connecticut (2005), as well as in Portland, Oregon, and Albuquerque, New Mexico (both in 2005).

A paper written in 2004 by three University of Wisconsin political scientists – Kenneth R. Mayer, Timothy Werner, and Amanda Williams – reports that "we do not yet have evidence that public funding has altered roll-call voting patterns or legislative coalitions...."[3] These authors, however, do provide evidence that the democratic process has been enriched in Arizona and Maine as a result of the adoption of full public funding for candidates. Clean elections have proved to be popular among candidates and, just as importantly, have reversed the downward trend in political competitiveness that had prevailed in those two states before the new system was implemented. The data in Tables 6.1 and 6.2 are the basis for

---

[3] Kenneth R. Mayer, Timothy Werner, and Amanda Williams, "Do Public Funding Programs Enhance Electoral Competition?" Paper presented at the Fourth Annual Conference on State Politics and Policy, Kent State University, April 30–May 1, 2004, updated March 2005, p. 23.

Table 6.1. Percentage of publicly funded candidates,
Maine and Arizona, 2000–2004

Year	Maine All Offices	Arizona Statewide Office	Arizona Legislative Districts
2000	33	43	28
2002	60	70	50
2004	78	86	55

Source: Steven M. Levin, *Keeping It Clean: Public Financing in American Elections* (Los Angeles: Center for Governmental Studies, 2006) pp. 39, 45.

Table 6.2. Percentage of incumbents in the
state house and assembly facing major party
challengers in general election 1990–2004

Year	Maine	Arizona
1990	83	NA
1992	78	NA
1994	71	48
1996	97	42
1998	81	40
2000	81	39
2002	91	57
2004	98	55

Source: Kenneth R. Mayer, Timothy Werner, and Amanda Williams, "Do Public Funding Programs Enhance Electoral Competition?" Paper Presented at the Fourth Annual Conference on State Politics and Policy, Kent State University, April 30–May 1, 2004, updated March 2005, Fig. 1.

the authors' conclusions that "there is no question that public funding programs have increased the pool of candidates willing and able to run for state legislative office" and that "public funding appears to have increased the likelihood that an incumbent will have a competitive race."[4] In short, the limited information available suggests that the election process has indeed been made more egalitarian in those states where an alternative to private funding is available.

The attractiveness of voluntary public funding of electoral campaigns seems likely to have been responsible for the fact that the percentage of incumbents facing major party challengers in general elections rose in the years after it was adopted. In Maine, this measure of competitiveness indicates that virtually every race in 2004 was contested, a remarkably high figure in light of the fact that as recently as 1994, more than one-fourth of the Maine elections were not contested. Similarly, in Arizona, the percentage of races that were contested in 2002 and 2004 averaged 56 percent compared to the 41 percent that was recorded in 1996 and 1998, the years immediately preceding the introduction of clean elections in that state.

These successes, however, have not yet been widely acknowledged. Long-standing arguments persist that suggest either the impracticality or the undesirability of clean

4 Ibid., p. 6.

elections. Two sets of objections – one from the political right and the other from the political left – typify those critiques.

On the right is the former chair of the Federal Elections Committee, Bradley A. Smith. Smith does not agree that political donors possess disproportionate power and influence. Though he concedes that campaign contributions "may play a role in a legislator's complex calculations of how to vote and what to say and do," he nonetheless finds "it implausible that this is really a major problem in American government." According to Smith, "the 'wealthy' do not vote with their dollars. All they can do with their dollars is attempt to persuade others how to vote. That is free speech and the essence of the First Amendment."[5]

Smith defends private campaign contributions as a form of democratic political participation. He writes that money " . . . is the single most important means by which people who lack talents with direct value in the political arena such as production of advertising, writing, campaign organization, speaking and the like can participate in politics beyond voting." Indeed, according to him, preventing such people from making political donations would be elitist. A ban on political contributions would favor "students and retirees, who have volunteer time over working people, who may have less time but more

---

[5] Bradley A. Smith, *Unfree Speech: The Folly of Campaign Finance Reform* (Princeton NJ, and Oxford: Princeton University Press, 2001), pp. 53, 55.

discretionary income. It favors persons who are skilled in producing political advertising over persons skilled in producing plastic injection-mold products. It favors skilled writers over skilled plumbers. But plumbers and owners of small injection-mold companies can participate effectively through money contributions."[6]

This argument concerning the democratic nature of private political financing is joined with a second proposition that seeks to narrow political equality as a concept. Because, writes Smith, "the very notion of politics presumes that some will have more influence than others," political equality does not mean "that each person has equal influence at all stages of the process, but that each has a right to vote and to have that vote weighted equally with those of others." Inequality of influence inevitably will be present in any political system because some citizens will chose while others will choose not to "use their differing abilities, financial wherewithal and personal disposition to become more or less active in political life and to attempt to persuade their fellow citizens to vote in a particular manner." The framers of the Constitution, Smith declares, "never intended that each person should have equal political influence." Thus, if campaign contributions were banned, " ... those with substantial influence beyond the act of voting will be drawn from a narrow caste of those with political skills"

[6] Ibid.,pp. 202, 204.

to the exclusion of "a wider group that includes those with money earned through nonpolitical talents."[7]

Smith's presentation is almost totally an exercise in question begging. The problem raised by a political system of private contributions is not whether political participation will be uneven throughout the population. Of course it will. Some people simply are not interested in politics. The question of importance – and the one Smith ignores – is whether those who are interested in influencing the political process beyond the act of voting possess a fair opportunity to do so under the current privately funded system. The answer is, they do not. With politicians dependent on private donations for their success, rich people potentially can contribute more money than other groups in society. They therefore are able to obtain a disproportionate claim on the recipient's time and attention. To be sure, office seekers have to be sensitive to the voters. But unless politicians prioritize their attention in the direction of the donor class, they will have no access to the electorate at all. Without money there can be no political campaigns, so those who make the campaigns possible have to be provided with privileged attention. Everyone else becomes a second-class citizen.

Smith stacks the deck by confining his sympathies to the plight of private donors who will be deprived of the use of their

---

[7] Ibid., pp. 210, 211.

wealth in politics. He expresses concern that in a system of public funding, an elite of students, retired people, and writers will exercise disproportionate influence. But no comparable expression of concern is voiced about the disproportionate influence exercised by wealthy individuals today.

The reality is that in a publicly funded political system, differences in power will emerge. Some individuals will be more influential than others. In the first place, wealth still will constitute an advantage. Clean elections systems are voluntary. Candidates still will be able to run for office using private funds, though of course it is likely that their doing so will become a political liability, exposing them to the charge of being the candidates of special interests. Furthermore, it will remain possible to use wealth to influence public opinion and thus indirectly shape the content of politics. A voluntary system of public funding for electoral campaigns is not a panacea. But it will make it more feasible for a wider spectrum of candidates and ideas to obtain a public hearing than is the case with a donor-driven system.

What differentiates the inequality that will prevail with public funding compared to the current system is that the differences in influence that will emerge will more likely be earned in debate, not bought. Some individuals, by virtue of their talents and powers of persuasion, will emerge as leaders. But that is no more than saying that the public will make choices in the political sphere. The difference will be that in the new system those choices will be made with the electorate selecting among candidates, each of whom has a roughly equal ability to present his or her case.

On the left, Samuel Bowles and Herbert Gintis deny that the economic sphere can successfully be walled off from the political realm in this way. They believe that creating political egalitarianism in association with a private property economy is a chimera. The gist of their argument is that corporate American will make it so costly for the electorate to reduce the role of private wealth in the political system that the public will be dissuaded from the effort. The weapon businesspeople will choose to make democracy unacceptably expensive is a "strike of capital."[8]

Bowles and Gintis argue that "capital has a kind of veto power over public policy that is quite independent of its ability to intervene directly in elections or in state decision making." As they put it, "the power of capital – its command over state policy – thus derives not so much from what it does but from what it might not do." And what it might not do is invest. Such a capital strike would occur, Bowles and Gintis theorize, in response to policies that threaten business profitability. That, in turn, would result in a damaging and unacceptable decline

---

[8] Quotations in the following two paragraphs come from Samuel Bowles and Herbert Gintis, *Democracy and Capitalism: Property, Community and the Contradictions of Modern Social Thought* (New York: Basic Books, 1987), p 88.

in production and a rise in unemployment, something most citizens would certainly wish to avoid.

Thus, from this perspective, it does not matter that elected officials directly depend on financial contributions made by representatives of businesses. Officeholders are forced to do what businesses want them to do in any case. If a government acted in a way that threatened profitability, the business community would retaliate by cutting back on their expenditures, thereby, as Bowles and Gintis put it, tending "to reduce the electoral prospects of the incumbent government." The power of the business community thus rests on its ability to "effectively (and without great cost) withdraw resources and thereby inflict large costs on an opponent." Thus, they conclude, "the presumed sovereignty of the democratic citizenry fails in the presence of capital strike."[9]

The problem with this argument is that it is driven by two assumptions that almost certainly are invalid. There is no justification for the belief that any government democratically responsive to its constituents will be hostile toward businesses. Similarly, it is far from obvious that a strike of capital will be the likely, if not the inevitable, response to the economic policies of a democratic government.

It simply is not reasonable to believe, as Bowles and Gintis do, that the electorate is and always will be unaware of,

[9]   Ibid., pp. 87, 90

dismissive of, or hostile to the fact that firms have to be profitable for economic growth and employment to be at high levels. Bowles and Gintis completely ignore the possibility that a business-friendly party, or at least a slate of politicians responsive to the needs of corporations, might be politically successful in a democratic environment. Similarly, they fail to provide any analysis concerning the threshold that would have to be breached for a capital strike to occur. In a country as rich as the United States, it would require a truly egregious and hostile set of policies for corporations to take the unprecedented step of pulling up stakes and abandoning the country, as Bowles and Gintis suggest might occur.[10]

The result of their one-sidedness in this regard is that Bowles and Gintis overstate both the political hostility to business firms and the negative corporate response that will be present in a clean elections system. Certainly there is nothing in the European experience of partial public political funding to suggest that the dire forebodings of Bowles and Gintis are valid. Similarly, in the clean elections states of Arizona and Maine, where most candidates pay for their campaigns with public funds, capitalism is not under siege, nor has a capital strike occurred.

It is probable that a more democratic politics than exists now would result in a reconfiguration of public policy toward

---

[10] Ibid., p. 88.

the economy. The current disproportionate influence of the corporate sector will be reduced. As a result, more extensive policies to protect workers from the dislocations associated with technological change and globalization could well be adopted. In such a political setting, there is also an enhanced likelihood that the country's system of health insurance will be improved and that more strenuous efforts will be made to protect the environment than is the case at present. But these are not the types of initiatives that are likely to trigger the kind of massive refusal by businesses to build productive capacity that Bowles and Gintis have in mind.

Still, there is the possibility that Bowles and Gintis may be right and that a government composed of clean legislators might overreach and trigger a hostile business response. Bowles and Gintis assume that under such circumstances it would be necessary to go through the time-consuming, costly, and disruptive process of constructing a new economic system.[11] That, however, would not be the only possibility or even the most likely one.

In a democratic setting, the consequences of economic policies would be under constant scrutiny and review. Undoubtedly in the kind of economic depression depicted by Bowles and Gintis, both publicly funded and privately funded candidates would voice their objections to policies that

[11] Ibid., pp. 89–90.

triggered the business community's hostile response. Those candidates could be depended on to propose alternatives. Their argument would be that policymakers had been insensitive to the requirements of a successful market economy and that the offending programs should be scaled back. If they were successful in convincing the electorate of their case, that opposition would emerge victorious in political campaigns. The policy innovations that caused the economic downturn would be scrapped and new programs adopted. If the political dissenters were not successful, those policies would remain in place, with the implicit message from the voters that they were willing to bear the costs of the disruptions such programs were causing.

With elections contested over how and in what direction to influence the economy, it is likely that what will emerge is a pattern of incremental adjustments. The debates will be over the extent to which corporations should benefit from privileges and incentives in order to encourage them to create wealth on the one hand, and the limits that should be imposed on such dispensations in the name of distributive justice on the other hand. How such debates will be resolved, of course, is unknowable. That will be decided by myriad conditions including the state of the economy to begin with and the persuasiveness of the participants in the discussions. But what could well develop among the people of the country is a more sophisticated appreciation of the economic choices

that confront society than is present now, when such deliberations are weighted to the interests of the business community
because of its role in providing campaign funds.

The arguments presented by Smith and by Bowles and
Gintis therefore both represent counsels of despair. Smith cannot foresee any way to curb the power of wealth without doing
violence to democratic processes. Bowles and Gintis believe
that business owners are so sensitive to their prerogatives
that the scope for democratic decision making in the political sphere is all but nonexistent.

The polarity represented by these conflicting views corresponds closely to the dichotomy that the political theorist John
Dunn finds recurring throughout the historical development
of democracy, dating back to the French Revoution. As Dunn
puts it, there was a "profound gulf between the true defenders
of equality and their sly and all too politically effective adversaries, the partisans of the order of egoism, or 'the English
doctrine of the economists.'" He refers to this conflict as one
between "the order of egoism," the defenders of the market,
and "the order of equality," those who rejected the market and
saw in egalitarianism "the consolation of the wretched." Dunn
writes that "the fundamental struggle on which the Revolution
had turned" was the fight between these two "orders."[12] From

---

[12] John Dunn, *Setting the People Free: The Story of Democracy* (London:
Atlantic Books, 2005), p. 124.

this perspective, Bradley A. Smith is aligned with the order of egoism, while Bowles and Gintis side with the defenders of equality.

According to Dunn, this conflict has played itself out repeatedly in the years since the beginning of the Age of Revolution in the late eighteenth century. Fundamentally, it is a disagreement over the role of the market in society. The conflict emerges because the market does not privilege equality, but instead is a mechanism to achieve efficiency and increase material prosperity. Indeed, according to Dunn, the market economy is "the most powerful mechanism for dismantling equality that humans have ever fashioned." Believing this, Dunn concludes that democracy, at least to the extent that the term connotes equality, "still clashes systematically and fundamentally with the defining logic of economic organization."[13]

Historically, the defenders of the order of egoism – the advocates of the market – have prevailed. The meaning of democracy, Dunn writes, "has passed definitively from the hands of the 'equals' to those of the political leaders of the order of egoism." Dunn is right in pointing out that "wherever the opportunity to vote freely has been extended across an adult population, the majority has found it unattractive to vote explicitly for the establishment of equality." For Dunn, as

[13] Ibid., pp. 124, 137, 187.

127

for us today, "the big question raised" by the acceptance of the market is "how much of the distant agenda of the order of equality can still be rescued from the ruins of its overwhelming defeat."[14]

Lying behind this popular rejection of the order of equality is undoubtedly the fact that the public has come to appreciate the economic accomplishments that can be achieved in societies that employ market mechanisms. It is only where markets are operative that modern economic growth has been achieved. That process, in turn, has been liberating. As Benjamin Friedman points out, economic development fosters "greater opportunity, tolerance of diversity, social mobility, commitment to fairness and dedication to democracy," all of which, he notes, are thought of positively in "explicitly moral terms."[15]

Since markets are instruments that produce inequality, but at the same time have the capacity, in appropriate circumstances, to greatly reduce deprivation, the terms of the argument have to be changed from those described by Dunn. Now the question turns out to be how much of the agenda of the order of equality should be saved and how much should be discarded in light of the fact that markets have an important role to play in achieving a just world. The fact is that the terms of the

[14] Ibid., pp. 160, 130, 145, 168.

[15] Benjamin M. Friedman, *The Moral Consequences of Economic Growth* (New York: Alfred A. Knopf, 2005), p. 4.

The Need for Public Financing

trade-off between growth and equality are not at all clear. Certainly it is not the case that anyone knows the optimal degree of inequality that is necessary to promote development. Similarly, no one knows precisely the level of egalitarianism that impedes development. The United States and the Netherlands have very different degrees of inequality, but the growth of their economies in recent years has been very similar.[16] In the most general terms, we know that markets do produce both inequality and growth, but beyond that there is a great deal of variance in practice and, as a result, even more theoretical uncertainty about how one affects the other.

Given this uncertainty, there is a need for a political system that provides the people of a society with the opportunity to choose among the options – the degree to which market mechanisms should be employed or rejected in the name of equality – that confront them. It is particularly important to construct such a system in a period of rapid change such as

---

[16] Between 1990 and 2003 the U.S. per capita gross national income, computed on a purchasing power parity basis, increased by 63.3 percent; the corresponding figure for the Netherlands was 61.6 percent. Computed from U.S. Census Bureau, *Statistical Abstract of the United States: 2006* (Washington, DC: Government Printing Office, 2005), Table 1327. Recent analyses comparing Europe and the United States have tended to conclude that the former's greater commitment to egalitarianism has not come at a substantial economic cost. See Joan Pontusson, *Inequality and Prosperity: Social Europe vs. Liberal America* (Ithaca, NY, and London: Cornell University Press, 2005), and Lane Kenworthy, *Egalitarian Capitalism: Jobs, Incomes and Growth in Affluent Countries* (New York: Russell Sage Foundation, 2004).

the current one. Technological change and globalization mean that a set of policies appropriate for one period might very well become inequitable in another.

The U.S. political system does not give its citizens a full opportunity to explore alternatives. Because of the way politics is paid for in this country, the entire range of options and policies are not made known. Approaches that are feasible are not presented – or at best are inadequately presented – due to the underfunding of candidacies that advocate them. They are sidestepped because of the damage they cause or threaten to cause to the interests of the donor elite.

That kind of implicit censorship could be minimized in a voluntary system of public financing of elections. In such a system, a wider array of candidates and perspectives would be presented than is the case now, when office seekers must trim their message to the shape of their patrons' political preferences. In such a setting, all that would be required to gain access to the ballot and thereby achieve a fair public hearing is passing a performance test – such as an agreed-on number of very low contributions – certifying at least a minimum level of political seriousness. With that, the political alternatives that will become part of the agenda for consideration almost certainly will be more extensive than is the case at present. And that is as it should be, given both the rapidity with which change is occurring in technological processes and the shape of the global economy.

7

Organizing for Democracy

The people of the United States have not adequately come to terms with the social and economic changes of the past thirty years. Globalization and computerization have been responsible for increased domestic income inequality. A plurality of Americans tells poll takers that they would like to see this trend offset and that the government should act to achieve greater equality. But the polling data also reveal widespread belief that the political system is rigged on behalf of the rich and that it is the elite who benefit from government initiatives. As a result, the public has not mobilized on behalf of redistributive programs, and the issue of inequality remains largely absent from the country's political agenda.

This lack of trust in the government, as Marc J. Hetherington points out, is "generally good news for those on the political right." As he puts it, "a low trust environment is ... advantageous for those who want government to do less." Since the right, he goes on, "opposes federal efforts at redistribution and extensions of the social safety net ... widespread political distrust aids these causes." Even so, Hetherington suggests that conservatives in general and Republicans in particular must take into account the latent support that persists for such programs. He goes so far as to maintain that "it is unclear whether conservative Republicans can continue to dominate the national government in the face of this opinion."[1]

However the situation plays out for the Republican Party, there can be no doubt that distrust of the government is much more of a problem for the political left than for the political right. The deep skepticism within the electorate about the intentions of the government has made it impossible for advocates of redistribution and active labor market interventions to prevail politically. As Hetherington puts it, "if progressives desire a change in the post-Watergate policy direction, they must start by finding a way to resuscitate the federal government's image." He writes, "progressives must make efforts to redefine what government means in the public mind, have the courage to praise the things it does well, and fight the urge to criticize its unpopular elements for political gain."[2]

Thus, for Hetherington, the problem for progressives becomes one of presentation. What he recommends is the articulation of "an alternative vision of government, as one

---

[1] Marc J. Hetherington, *Why Trust Matters: Declining Political Trust and the Demise of American Liberalism* (Princeton, NJ, and Oxford: Princeton University Press, 2005), p. 142, 143, 145.

[2] Ibid., pp. 145, 146.

that takes care of older Americans, protects the environment, builds highways and the like. " What he wants to do is induce Americans to evaluate government positively, using favorable rather than unfavorable images. Discussions of the government should shift away from association with welfare programs. Instead, he writes, progressives should embrace "patriotic symbols and a strong military" as well as raising "the profile of government's successes" with Social Security and Medicare.[3]

Hetherington is not the only one making suggestions to progressives about presentation. George Lakoff has come to prominence making the same kind of argument. In his formulation, what is crucial in politics is how positions are "framed." Lakoff believes that politics in the United States is organized around two opposite and idealized models of the family. The model that is consistent with the worldview of the left is the "nurturant parent model," while the "strict father model" corresponds to the conservative worldview. Political competition, for Lakoff, is fundamentally about which side can evoke its preferred model more successfully in the minds of the electorate.[4]

What is critical for Lakoff is the frame used in presenting issues. In countering the positions adopted by the right, Lakoff suggests that the phrase "stronger America" be used to counter the conservatives' use of "strong defense." This formulation is

---

[3] Ibid., p. 146.

[4] George Lakoff, *Don't Think of an Elephant: Know Your Values and Frame the Debate* (White River Junction, VT: Chelsea Green, 2004), pp. 39, 40.

more likely, he believes, to evoke a nurturant rather than a martial impulse. In a list that he provides, he recommends "broad prosperity" to stand in opposition to "free markets," "better future" instead of "lower taxes," "effective government" rather than "smaller government," and "mutual responsibility" as an offset to "family values." In all of this, Lakoff urges progressives to formulate the discussion of specific issues in a way that will evoke a response favorable to the position adopted by the left.[5]

In these discussions of presentation, the role of the donor elite in shaping the political agenda is little more than an afterthought. Campaign funding is not even mentioned in the book Lakoff intended "to be a practical guide for both citizen activists and for anyone with a serious interest in politics."[6] Hetherington mentions the need for campaign finance reform on only one page in his book. But even there, it is discussed not because it will bring with it a necessary change in the structure of politics, but only because it will make it more likely that the electorate will perceive Democrats favorably.[7] In neither book is campaign finance reform considered a central issue facing progressives. These authors do not engage the reality that the political power of wealth is debilitating to the liberal cause.

The handicap is particularly powerful with regard to the problem of increasing income inequality. It is hard to envision

---

[5] Ibid., p. 94
[6] Ibid., p. xv.
[7] J. Hetherington, *Why Trust Matters*, p. 149.

the inequities caused by globalization and new technologies being offset with the current political funding system. The agenda-setting power of wealth is so great that it prevents a serious consideration of redistributive policies. Without a dramatic diminution in that power, little can be expected. While in principle the government could, as the liberal columnist E. J. Dionne, Jr., would have it do, throw its weight "on the side of those in the middle class and those less well off who are trying to advance their interests and those of their children,"[8] the reality is that because of the way politics is paid for, this is unlikely to occur. With this the case, the electorate's cynicism probably corresponds more closely to the reality than does the hope of liberals that they will be able to deliver on the income-transferring and labor market support policies that globalization requires. Democrats, after all, did control the House of Representatives continuously from 1960 through 1994 and the Senate in all of those years except those between 1980 and 1986, but they did little to curb growing inequality. Indeed, since campaign expenditures began to shoot out of sight and dependence on donor funding of campaigns intensified, no new big social programs have been adopted. The last of these, Medicare, was adopted more than forty years ago, in 1965. What is at issue here is the fact that progressives and liberals have not

---

[8] E. J. Dionne, Jr., *Stand Up, Fight Back*, (New York: Simon & Schuster, 2004), p. 200.

assigned a high enough priority to the role played by wealth in shaping the content of politics. The problem is more substantive that the advocates of a progressive framing strategy would have it.

Neither of the two major pieces of campaign finance reform legislation that have been adopted over the past thirty years has solved the problem. Despite FECA and BCRA, private wealth retains its power in the political system. The form and pattern of contributions may have changed at the margin, but no one doubts that rich white conservative men still provide the overwhelming amount of the money that politicians require for their campaigns. The donors and their business interests still benefit from a level of political responsiveness that is denied to the rest of the population. As a result, as Zelizer puts it, election financing "reform failed to end public distrust of campaigns."[9]

Notwithstanding this judgment, Zelizer himself is careful not to evaluate the reform movement too harshly, writing that "the accomplishments of the reform coalition should not be discounted." In particular, he argues that "there was a revolution in disclosure of political information." He reminds his readers that until the 1960s, little was known about political contributions. He credits the reform activists with creating "a more transparent and porous process where single

[9] Julian E. Zelizer, "Seeds of Cynicism: The Struggle Over Campaign Finances, 1956–1974," in Paula Baker (ed.), *Money and Politics* (University Park: Pennsylvania State University Press, 2002), p. 75.

contributors could no longer dominate the system without public knowledge."[10] In this regard, it is important to point out that the new technology, specifically the Internet, has provided an important vehicle for this increased transparency. The Federal Election Commission (FEC) routinely posts its reports on its website. Using the data thus supplied, the Center for Responsive Politics, on its website, offers invaluable analysis of the sources and beneficiaries of private political contributions. Even here, however, the results are ambiguous. It is at least arguable that increased knowledge about the nature and sources of campaign contributions may have been one of the roots of increased political cynicism. Knowledge of the size of the problem may contribute to despair rather than remedial activism.

At the heart of the coalition that lobbied successfully for both FECA and BCRA was Common Cause, founded in 1970 by the former secretary of health, education and welfare in the Johnson administration, John Gardner. Neither of those pieces of legislation matched Gardner's ambitions. From the first, he called for the public funding of election campaigns. In 1973, for example, Gardner told the House Administration Committee that "Common Cause believes that the root of campaign finance [abuse] can never be eliminated until candidates are assured of adequate funds to run a credible and competitive

[10]   Ibid., p. 104.

campaign without having to rely on big-money contributors. This can never be accomplished until a comprehensive system of public financing is adopted."[11]

Common Cause was a "citizen's lobby," the pioneer organization pressuring the Congress to adopt reform. Using a computer-based direct mail drive, Common Cause, in the words of Robert E. Mutch, created a "nationwide membership organization without ever leaving Washington, DC." He goes on, "by directing the mailings to well-educated people in the upper reaches of the income distribution . . . Common Cause attracted members able and eager to finance a fully staffed national office and several state branches." Within six months there were 100,000 Common Cause members and, by the beginning of 1972, nearly 250,000. As Mutch summarizes the situation as it existed in the early 1970s, "until Watergate there had been no effective constituency for campaign finance reform; Common Cause provided one for the first time."[12]

And indeed, during 1974 in the aftermath of Watergate, it looked as if there was a realistic chance of passing legislation to allow for the public funding of congressional races. In April of that year, the Senate passed a bill to that effect for both primary and general elections. Under the legislation, candidates,

[11] Quoted in Steven M. Gillon, *That's Not What We Meant to Do: Reform and Its Unintended Consequences in Twentieth-Century America* (New York: W. W. Norton, 2000), p. 201.

[12] Robert E. Mutch, *Campaigns, Congress and Courts: The Making of Federal Campaign Finance Law* (New York: Praeger, 1988), p. 44.

in exchange for such funding, would accept strict spending and contribution limits. Furthermore, it appeared that such legislation enjoyed public support. Gillon reports that two-thirds of those polled in a survey in that year supported public financing of election campaigns.[13]

The companion bill in the House of Representatives, however, did not contain the provision for public funding of congressional candidates. When supporters of public funding in that chamber attempted to amend the bill to include the provision, they were defeated by a 228–187 vote, and as the legislation was finally adopted, public financing remained omitted. What did pass was a system of public funding for the presidential campaign, and it may be that this is what Gardner had in mind when he was reported as saying that with FECA "we got more than we had expected other than in the area of public financing of federal congressional elections."[14]

As it turned out, this was the legislative high water mark with regard to public financing of elections. At no point since then has public funding of congressional elections come as close to adoption as it did then. In short, the opportunity provided by Watergate came and went. Since then, advocates for congressional clean elections have not been able to reclaim the political salience that they possessed in those years.

---

[13] Gillon, *That's Not What We Meant to Do*, pp. 201, 203.
[14] Ibid., p. 209.

What it would have taken to do so is, of course, a question that is impossible to answer. This strategic problem was hard in any case. But the difficulty of devising a plan that would rekindle interest in electoral reform was compounded by the new political consensus that emerged in the country. During the 1980s, with the advent of the Reagan administration, the desirability of downsizing the public sector became part of the country's political conventional wisdom. The view that the size and role of government should be reduced directly contradicted the idea that tax revenues should be used to assist political office seekers. Clean elections advocates faced very powerful headwinds.

But it is also true that the reform movement failed to respond adequately to the changed circumstances in which it existed. In particular, it failed to transcend the limits that defined its initial success. Created as an organization of the relatively privileged middle class, Common Cause did not, during these years of increased income inequality, adjust its message. It did not adequately identify the role private political contributions played in limiting governmental policies to offset that trend. More generally, it did not convince the public that for the government to become a servant of the population in general rather than a tool of special interests, elected officials had to be freed from their dependence on private patrons.

At least in part, this weakness stemmed from the fact that from the start, Common Cause was conceived as a citizen lobbying organization, oriented to pressuring members of Congress to pass reform legislation. It did not see itself as the leader of a social movement. It was a membership organization, but its members were not called on to do much besides signing up and paying their dues. The organization's strategy was to lobby members of Congress assuming that membership numbers would provide the clout necessary to win Congress over to reform. It believed that its goals could be attained without an activist presence at the grassroots level.

It is, of course, true that Common Cause sought to become as large as it could. Lawrence C. Rothenberg cites one of its officers as saying that "We want to make Common Cause membership as available to as wide a spectrum as we can." To this end, the organization's dues were kept relatively low. But the fact remains that much more of its resources were devoted to policy development and lobbying efforts than were used to nurture local and regional chapters. The organization in fact did very little face-to-face grassroots direct organizing. Rothenberg writes, "for Common Cause the likelihood of being asked to join is virtually tantamount to whether one receives a mail solicitation."[15] Throughout much of its history, the leaders of the organization probably agreed with Skocpol's 2003 assessment: "Common Cause has managed to do quite well,

---

[15] Lawrence S. Rothenberg, *Linking Citizens to Government: Interest Group Politics at Common Cause* (New York: Cambridge University Press, 1992), p. 71.

thank you, with several hundred thousand ... relatively privileged and sophisticated supporters. The organization really has little need to dig deeper for many times more 'members.' "[16]

If the only criterion to be used in assessing Common Cause was the ability of the organization to sustain itself, this favorable judgment might be acceptable. But it is clear that its leaders and members, as well as those of similar like-minded groups such as Public Campaign, seek something more than organizational viability. They seek change in the American political system, and that they have failed to accomplish. The inequality in the political system caused by the fact that political campaigns are paid for with privately donated funds remains. Solving that problem will require mobilization of the American people on behalf of reform on a scale far beyond what these organizations have been so far able to achieve.

Such a mobilization will require that reform activists take advantage, to a degree far greater than they have to date, of the issue's one unshakable strength. There are few social problems whose remedies do not have to confront the power and opposition of wealth. If advocates for the arts seek public funds, they must contend with the political aversion of the wealthy to taxation. If grassroots organizations oppose the granting of tax benefits to special interests, they must fight an uphill battle against

[16] Theda Skocpol, *Diminished Democracy: From Membership to Management in American Society* (Norman: University of Oklahoma Press, 2003), p. 224.

well-funded adversaries. If alternative energy advocates seek legislation, they must contend with officeholders beholden to giant petroleum corporations. Crop subsidies persist, at least in part, because food processing and marketing conglomerates provide funding to congressional officeholders. Creating an efficient and effective health care system requires overcoming the vested interests of insurance companies and large pharmaceutical houses. The list can be extended virtually without limit. The point is that, potentially, there is a very wide community of people whose interests and political concerns would be advanced if the role of private money in politics were reduced. There is, in short, a wide potential constituency for electoral reform, but the reform movement has not yet devised an effective strategy to mobilize that latent support.

The breadth of potential support is particularly extensive if the inequality associated with technological change and globalization is included. The transformations occurring at the workplace and in the international economy in recent years have sharply divided the U.S. labor force into two groups: those who have benefited from those changes and those whose interests have been damaged. This trend toward inequality, as we have seen, is deeply rooted and is not likely to reverse itself. At the same time, there is ample scope for governmental interventions to ameliorate the injustices that have resulted. But the donor elite, by and large, stands in opposition to such efforts, and that opposition will have to be neutralized politically if a just domestic response to changing technology and globalization is to become a reality.

At the moment, prospects are not bright. The public seems stuck. People report that they would like something to be done about inequality, but they are reluctant to press the government to intervene. They rightly suspect that officeholders do not assign their concerns a high priority. If something were done to overcome those misgivings, then a large political constituency might well be mobilized on behalf of redistributive policies. But until that occurs, not much is likely to change.

Campaign reform advocates possess the policy key in this regard. A skeptical electorate might well be won over to egalitarian interventions and policies if it were convinced that politicians really were seeking to represent their interests. If elected officials were perceived as no longer beholden to financial patrons, voters could well rethink their ambivalence concerning public sector economic interventions. The prospect of a publicly funded political legislature in Washington, with its responsiveness to wealth minimized, might come to be thought of as a potential ally rather than an enemy in reversing the trend toward inequality.

This said, however, it is obvious that the campaign reform community is not yet in a position to make this case to the wider public. It does not possess deep roots anywhere but among the strata of well-educated individuals from which it emerged. Neither Common Cause nor other similar organizations have successfully done the kind of cross-class grassroots organizing and membership building that would provide it with a credible presence in any other population segment.

There is much in American life, of course, that discourages grassroots organizing and civic engagement. Robert Putnam is the most prominent of numerous observers who have commented on, and expressed regret about, this development.[17] Thus, it is easy to suggest that it is futile to try to organize activism with a membership-based organization. Face-to-face politics are thought to be passé, a phenomenon of a bygone day. But while this may be the conventional wisdom, the same technologies that lie at the root of the trend toward inequality may yet provide the means by which to rehabilitate participatory politics.

Thus, Joe Trippi, Howard Dean's campaign manager in the 2004 Democratic Party primary races, recounts how the Internet can be used to bring people together and, in the process, empower them in ways that encourage both participation and creativity. In this case, a website was used to match people politically and give them a time and a place to meet. Trippi reports that most such meetings were small. But he nonetheless argues that this represented the use of "technology as a way for people of similar interests, passions and causes to find each

---

[17] Robert D. Putnam, *Bowling Alone: The Collapse and Revival of American Community* (New York: Simon and Schuster, 2000). See also Skocpol, *Diminished Democracy.*

other and *instantly* form into communities...."[18] Beyond simply facilitating discussion, the new technology could be put to use as a force for renewed involvement and participation.

Trippi himself is prone to overstatement concerning the Internet, as when he calls the Dean campaign "a stunning victory" that was "the opening salvo in a revolution, the sound of hundreds of thousands of Americans turning off their televisions and embracing the only form of technology that has allowed them to be involved again...." Nevertheless, he is on to something important when he remarks that while the present era is often referred to as the "information age," he believes that "what we're really in now is *the empowerment age*." As he puts it, "if information is power then this new technology – which is the first to evenly distribute information – is really distributing power." For Trippi, "the Internet is the last hope for democracy."[19]

Because Trippi's enthusiasm is so infectious, it is easy to forget that in the Dean campaign the new technology was used to do what all privately funded campaigns have to do – raise money. And while Trippi argues that raising money in relatively limited amounts from small donors was an important way to mobilize Dean supporters – differentiating the Dean

---

[18] Joe Trippi, *The Revolution Will Not Be Televised: Democracy, the Internet and the Overthrow of Everything* (New York: Regan Books, 2004), p. 84; emphasis in original.

[19] Ibid., p. xviii, 4; emphasis in original.

candidacy from others – the fact remains that almost two-fifths (39 percent) of the money Dean raised came from donors who gave \$200 or more.[20] Technology alone does not ensure a politics insulated from the disproportionate influence of wealth.

An alternative model is presented by a campus-based organization called Democracy Matters,[21] which uses the new technology to generate political energy on behalf of the public funding of elections. In this case, the Internet and email are used to build Democracy Matters chapters at individual colleges and universities, with the expectation that political activism will be generated in local clubs. Democracy Matters groups form coalitions with school and community reform activists, hoping to convince people that electoral reform is the gateway issue to other progressive causes. There is also the expectation that students who become politically engaged on campus will become the next generation of political leaders in support of enriching the democratic process.

Democracy Matters employs paid student interns on each campus to organize its chapters and mentors these individuals using both the organization's website and email, as well as the old-fashioned methods of staff visits and telephone calls. The success of the organization – at this writing it is completing its sixth year in operation and over those years has been present

---

[20] Center for Responsive Politics, 2004 Donor Demographics, http://www.opensecrets.org.

[21] Currently, I am the treasurer of Democracy Matters.

on more than seventy-five campuses per year – indicates that Trippi is right about the accomplishments that can be achieved with the new technology. But what he does not emphasize enough is that to realize its potential, face-to-face organizing efforts are also necessary.

Because Common Cause and the other campaign finance reform organizations have not attempted to create local groups and chapters, we cannot generalize from the Democracy Matters experience. Although the issue of money in politics has been around for a long time, its viability as an issue around which to organize at the grassroots level has not been seriously tested. In politics, if no one is talking about an issue, it tends to lie moribund. And so, the fact that clean elections is not a topic prominently debated and does not appear near the top of the list when people rank the issues that concern them signals political failure. To overcome that failure, it will be necessary to recruit and organize people around the issue, and in general that has not yet occurred.

What is possible to report on is the experience of Democracy Matters in this regard, and it is quite instructive. There is a significant on-campus constituency attracted to this issue. What moves most of the young people who are involved with Democracy Matters is the elementary issue of political fairness. They are outraged by the gross unfairness of the political system. They do not believe that wealth should be the currency of political influence. Most of these students believe that a democracy should imply political equality and that public financing is the best means to achieve that equality.

It may be true that a similar attitude prevails among adults. We do not know, because so little effort has been made to work with the public on this issue. But the fact that such a stance exists among young people makes it seem likely that that is the case. The same argument that is made on campus in the name of political equality may work off campus as well. If so, there is the potential for a broad-based political movement to develop in the name of democracy. What it awaits is the commitment of political activists and organizers.

If such a movement did exist, it is all but certain that debates among activists would not be confined to the installation of public funding systems. There would also be discussions concerning the kinds of policies that should be adopted under a new, more democratic regime. And the same widening of debate would be likely to occur if public funding of candidates were actually adopted. The national political agenda would be expanded by the existence of a reform movement and even more so if this movement were successful in achieving its objective.

By the very nature of an egalitarian political process, the outcome of those deliberations has to be considered open-ended. What emerges is contingent on the nature of the debates and the concerns of the participants. But precisely because the interests of all would be represented, it seems highly likely that the configuration of the policies that emerge will differ significantly from those that are implemented at present. In particular, the interests of people victimized by technological progress and globalization will certainly be articulated more in those circumstances than is the case now. To the extent that those interests are represented and spoken for, the one-sided, imbalanced impact of modern technology would likely be adjusted.

Globalization and technological change can be made more fair, but for that to occur, the voices of people who are put at risk by those processes have to be heard. A grassroots organizing effort holds out the promise that a political system that embodies equality can be achieved. If that is so, there is also hope that the damaging impetus to increased economic inequality can be abated.

Index

Aaron, Henry J., 9*t*, 29*t*
abortion, 55*n*12, 77–8
access to candidates, donor, 93
activism, 4, 68–9, 99, 136–50
Adema, Willem, 31*t*, 32*n*1
advertising, 67, 74–8, 138
  as freedom of speech, 70–1,
    117
  "magic words" requirement
    in, 73, 77
  television, 66, 69, 75–6, 87–8
advocacy, advertising, 73, 74–6,
  77–8
African Americans, 44
Aid to Families with Dependent
  Children (AFDC), 46
Alesina, Alberto, 44–5
Alexander, Herbert E., 65–7,
  69*n*13
American National Election
  Studies, 100–7

American Political Science
  Association (APSA), 89–96
apathy, 66–7, 135, 137
  and trust in government,
    99–107, 131–2, 144
Arizona, "clean elections" in,
  114–17, 123
Asia, 14, 17–20, 24, 25
attitudes, donor and voter
  globalization, 38–42, 143–4
  public financing of
    campaigns, 139
  redistributive programs, 44–9,
    58–60
  trust in government, 99–107

Baker, Paul, 62*n*2, 68*n*12
Balint, Peter J., 37
Bangladesh, 17
Bartels, Larry M., 94
Baumol, William J., 20*n*8

Index

Bergsten, C. Fred, 19*n*7, 35*n*4, 36*n*6

Bipartisan Campaign Reform Act (BCRA), 74–82, 136–8

Blinder, Alan S., 24

Bowles, Samuel, 121–6, 127

Bradford, Scott C., 19*n*7

Brady, Henry E., 52–3

Brazil, 24

broadcast advertising, 75–6

Buckley v. Valeo, 69–70, 73

Burtless, Gary, 9*t*, 29*t*

business sector, 13, 77, 78, 95, 110–12

  donations from, 54–60, 63, 66, 72, 74–6, 136

  response to "clean elections," 121–6

cable advertising, 75–6

campaign contributions

  defined, 72–82

  donor expectations and profiles, 52–66, 69, 88–98, 100–7, 136, 140

  as form of free speech, 70–1, 117

  Howard Dean campaign, 146–8

  2008 elections, 50*n*5

  see also attitudes, donor and voter; wealth, power of; *name of sector*

campaign finance reform

  "clean elections," 114–26, 139–40, 148

  grassroots mobilization for, 4, 68–9, 99, 136–50

  legislation, 67–81, 136, 137, 139

campaign financing, 49–54, 72

  corruption in, 62–4, 70, 76, 86, 89–93, 95

  history of, 61–7

  mass media and, 50*t*, 51, 52, 54*t*

  role of Internet in, 145–8

  see also advertising; public financing of campaigns

Canada, 15

Cantor, Joseph E., 72*n*16, 75*n*20

capital, 110, 111, 121–6

Census, U.S. Department of, 129*n*16

Center for Responsive Politics, 55–7, 79–81, 83*t*, 137, 147*n*20

China, 17–19, 24, 25

civil service employees, 55*n*12, 62–4

Index

Index

Index

Index

Index

Index

Index

public policy, 36–42, 43–4,
89–100
public sector, 49, 55*n*12, 62–4,
132–4, 140
trust in, 99–107, 131–2, 144
public spending, earmarks for,
92, 97–8
Putnam, Robert D., 145

racism, 44
radio advertising, 66
Rawls, John, 2, 3–4, 111–12
real estate industry, 58
redistributive programs, 27–36
attitudes toward, 44–9, 58–60
desired outcomes for, 98–107
mobilization for, 131, 143–4
re-framing of, 131–6
reform, *see* campaign finance
reform
regulated contributions, *see*
hard money
religious groups, 55*n*12
Republican Party, 56*t*, 57–8,
61–5, 73–4, 132
restricted contributions, *see*
hard money
retirees, 55*n*12
rhetoric, political parties and,
132–4
Richardson, J. David, 36

right, political, 59, 98, 117–21,
126, 132–4
Rosen, Howard, 35–6, 37
Rothenberg, Lawrence C., 141

Sacerdote, Bruce, 44–5
satellite advertising, 75–6
Scheve, Kenneth F., 38–40, 41
Schlozman, Kay Lehman,
52–3
Schuh, Scott, 21–2
self-interest, campaign
contributions and, 69,
88–98
service sector, 35, 54–60, 58
Sierra Club, 55*n*12
Sifrey, Micah L., 94–5
skills, *see* job skills and training
Skocpol, Theda, 141–2
Slaughter, Matthew J., 38–40,
41
Smeeding, Timothy M., 10–13,
15, 17
Smith, Bradley A., 117–21, 126,
127
Smith, David A., 44*n*1
social programs, 8–13, 30–3, 59,
94–5
see also redistributive
programs
soft money, 72–82

Index

Sorauf, Frank J., 61–2, 66–7, 68*n*9

special interests, 52–66, 100–7, 113, 136, 140
  see also name of sector

speech, free, campaign financing as, 70–1, 117

Stanley, Harold W., 74*t*, 97*n*8, 105*n*14

"strike of capital," 121–6

students, organizing of, 147–9

Summers, Mark Wahlgren, 62–3

Supreme Court, U.S., 69–78, 86

surveys, *see* attitudes, donor and voter

Sweden, 15, 30

Task Force on American Democracy in the Age of Rising Inequality (APSA), 89–96

taxes, 8–10, 12–13, 30–2, 47, 59, 95
  see also public financing of campaigns

tax-exempt organizations, 55–6, 71–2, 74–5, 78–81, 83*t*

technological change
  computerization, 14, 16, 17, 131, 145–8

effects on globalization, 13–17, 27–8

growth of international trade, 19–25

public policy response to, 36–7, 98–100

public response to, 38–42, 143–4
  see also education; job skills and training

technology, role in political participation, 145–8

television advertising, 66, 69, 75–6, 87–8

Thiess-Morse, Elizabeth, 103–5

Thurow, Lester C., 38

trade, 18–25, 34–42

Trade Adjustment Assistance (TAA), 34–5, 41

training, *see* job skills and training

"transactional lobbying," 92–3, 104

transfer policies and programs, 12–13, 44, 45
  see also redistributive programs

Triest, Robert K., 21–2

Trippi, Joe, 145–8, 148

trust in government, 99–107, 131–2, 144

Index

Index